A bold new approach to solving your own problems and stimulating creative solutions in others.

Gerard I. Nierenberg's startling new self-advisory techniques pave the way inside your everyday way of thinking . . . to a virtually limitless font of wisdom and creative problem-solving. You'll never think the same way again!

Praise for bestselling author and master negotiator Gerard I. Nierenberg:

"Gerard I. Nierenberg, author of *The Art of Negotiating,* makes a profession of trying to convince adversaries that nobody has to lose."
— *The Wall Street Journal*

"A JACK OF ALL NEGOTIATING TRADES—HIS CLIENT FILE READS LIKE A LIST OF FORTUNE 500 COMPANIES . . . Nierenberg has built a successful business teaching the techniques of negotiating to major corporations, trade groups, and other organizations."
— Associated Press

"THANK YOU FOR THESE INSIGHTS—Your books on negotiating have provided invaluable background information on the fundamentals of negotiating, and, moreover, have led to many new ways of thinking about the whole U.S.–U.S.S.R. negotiating relationship."
— James A. Miller, Captain, USAF
Special Assistant to the Joint Chiefs of Staff
Representative for SALT

"MY THANKS—the reaction of the students to your presentation was overwhelmingly favorable. Most of the students thought it was the best program they had ever encountered at Goddard."
— Carl A. Mohwinkel, Employee Development Specialist,
NASA Goddard Space Flight Center

"AN AMERICAN NEGOTIATING GURU WHO HAS PREACHED HIS PHILOSOPHY TO 65,000 PEOPLE AROUND THE WORLD."
— *Canada Financial Times*

Even when you do consult with an outside expert, *You're the Expert* will empower you to become a better prepared, insightful, and above all *successful* businessperson, patient, or client.

Berkley Books by Gerard I. Nierenberg

THE COMPLETE NEGOTIATOR
YOU'RE THE EXPERT

YOU'RE THE EXPERT:

HOW YOU CAN SOLVE YOUR PROBLEMS IN BUSINESS AND IN LIFE

GERARD I. NIERENBERG

Published in hardcover as *How to Give Yourself Good Advice*

Revised edition

BERKLEY BOOKS, NEW YORK

Published in hardcover as *How to Give Yourself Good Advice*

This Berkley book contains the complete
text of the original hardcover edition.

YOU'RE THE EXPERT

A Berkley Book / published by arrangement with
the author

PRINTING HISTORY
Nierenberg & Zeif Publishers edition published 1986
Berkley trade paperback edition / December 1991

ISBN: 0-425-13082-7

A BERKLEY BOOK ® TM 757,375
Berkley Books are published by The Berkley Publishing Group,
200 Madison Avenue, New York, New York 10016.
The name "BERKLEY" and the "B" logo
are trademarks belonging to Berkley Publishing Corporation.

PRINTED IN THE UNITED STATES OF AMERICA

10 9 8 7 6 5 4 3 2 1

In memory of my mother,
Sally Nierenberg

Contents

x

Introduction

When asked at one of my seminars how I had come to write so many books, I was forced to answer that when someone asks me a question I can't answer, I write a book.

No seminar is concluded without many attendees asking over and over: *Where* can I find an expert? *Who* should be asked? *What* shall I do? Understanding how limited my answers were, I realized it was again time for "that" book. Although in each case I had given my best advice, would I have taken the advice and would I have asked myself? My first approach was *How to Give and Receive Advice*. Now this new edition.

The entire advice process is rampant with doubts. Maybe this is as it should be. Some of my present conclusions contained in this book are based on the fact that you often give yourself very good advice. Now then, how can you maximize the results?

How can you avoid casting the same doubts on your own advice that you do on advice received from others? Can you distinguish the differences and then utilize them?

In the first century B.C., Publilius Syrus wrote: "Many receive advice; few profit from it." There are many reasons for this. Much advice that is given is in reality a command; "Do this or you'll lose out on a great deal." No wonder intelligent people often rebel against would-be advisers. They don't want to be "told" what to do; they want

1

to arrive at a rational and possibly beneficial decision that only they can make.

This book does not attempt to steer you to the "expert" givers of advice. They can be found everywhere you look, and you can stop and listen at your own risk. Instead, many contrasting life situations are presented to encourage self-awareness, initiate thought, and stimulate growth. Even the chapters are divided into the ends we seek or wish to avoid, and opposite methods and philosophies we might want to consider are shown.

Stories, anecdotes, news items, common experiences, and "morals" are also presented, not as "facts" or as gems of wisdom, but rather as statements to sensitize your imagination and force your deep-seated experiences to the surface, to make you think. The goal is in accord with Cicero's advice, "No one can give you wiser advice than yourself."

I
Success

Success Sits Fickly on One's Shoulder

Success is something you might talk about later, but to achieve it, action in the present is vital. Life does not provide us with a constant stream of opportunities to become successful, but when they arise, we should be prepared to seize and act on them. An elderly lion, Frasier, was a case in point. Frasier was 17 to 20 years old—the equivalent of 85 to 100 years in a human being. He hung around a California animal sanctuary, apparently, like many retirees, anticipating the end and a decent burial. A UPI correspondent, Barney Seibert, described him as "so old his tongue muscles have collapsed and his tongue lolls constantly from his mouth. He walks with difficulty and can no longer lead the hunt."

Frasier's rise to fame and success was sudden and unexpected. The sanctuary had 11 lionesses who refused to mate with the young lions that were provided. Sometimes they badly mauled their eager suitors. Noting that the lionesses were at least tolerant of Frasier, the staff decided to give him a chance. "Next morning the lionesses were found purring contentedly in the sun about an exhausted but happy Frasier, who lay on his back, paws in the air, tongue protruding." In the remaining two years of his life, Frasier sired a number of cubs by his pride of lionesses. And they were grateful. When he was hungry they fetched him food and laid it at his feet. When he walked, a lioness walked on either side of him to prop him up. Frasier returned the favors. One skeptic counted 26 matings in a single afternoon and then gave up counting. When Frasier died, he left behind him 35 children and 1 grandchild. One of his wives was still pregnant. Not a bad record for a so-called has-been who was open to his opportunity when it came to him. After his death, however, another zoo reported that Frasier's father was still alive and still siring cubs.

Moral: No matter how successful you are, someone will still try to outdo you.

Success as a Plus or Minus

Porfirio Salinas, a painter of Texas landscapes, became an instant success during the Johnson administration when Mrs. Johnson commissioned him to paint some of her husband's favorite scenes. Five of his works hung in the private quarters of the White House, and this was enough to send the prices of his pictures soaring. John Connally, then Governor of Texas, asked the artist's agent, "Has he started painting better?" The agent didn't think he had. "Then his paintings aren't worth any more now, either," Connally retorted. The agent later said, "I found it difficult to argue with such clearheaded and impeccable logic, however wrong it might be." Connally, of course, was wrong. Success had added an extra dimension to the artist's reputation and increased the monetary value of his works.

Moral: Success is the total of many things.

Sometimes too much success can lead to unexpected results. In 1938 MGM released *Boys Town*, a movie about Father Flanagan (played by Spencer Tracy) begging, borrowing, and paying to keep his idea alive. It was to offer a nonsectarian home for homeless and neglected boys. The movie and its sequel ensured the success of a mammoth fundraising effort on behalf of Boys Town. Some 30 million solicitation letters went out each year, and millions of dollars in donations came back. The director who had succeeded Father Flanagan said, "In the twenty-five years I have been the director, I've tried in every possible way to increase the amount of money Boys Town receives, with the help of the Morgan Guaranty Trust Company of New York."

In 1972, the Sun Newspapers of Omaha published an eight-page section entitled "Boys Town, America's Wealthiest City?" In it, Boys Town's net worth was set at more than $209 million. Its population of 993 meant it had a net worth of more than $200,000 per person. After that, contributions dropped drastically, and a new director was confronted with the problem of choosing new goals beyond that of "making a lot of money."

Moral: We may limit success by the goals we set.

How to Recognize Success

Some people base their judgments of success on quantity rather than quality. "More" for them is "better," although they never come to grips with the question: Better than what? These are the people who, when they see a crowded parking lot around a discount center, say, "That store must be making a lot of money." Not necessarily so. The only valid observation that can be made is that there are a large number of cars parked in the lot. Only the profit-and-loss sheet of the discount firm can tell you whether it is making money, and even this must be viewed with extreme caution and verified in several different ways.

The Equity Funding Corporation of America scandal in the 1970's is instructive. Take only two aspects of the case: Equity Funding claimed it had $25 million in negotiable bonds at a Chicago bank, but when the Illinois Insurance Department belatedly investigated, it found the safety deposit box empty. Equity also "created" 56,000 fake life insurance policies and sold them to overtrusting big-name insurers. And not only were 56,000 policies created; so were 56,000 nonexistent policyholders who lived and died, paid premiums, and defaulted on them in the same proportions as their real-life counterparts. Auditors, reinsurers, watchdog agencies, and the public were all fooled. Stock-market analysts recommended Equity stock as "a Buy." If any of them had taken the trouble to read Nikolai Gogol's

Dead Souls, they would not have been deceived so easily. In that book an unscrupulous adventurer journeyed throughout Russia buying title to "dead souls"—serfs whose names had appeared on the preceding census lists but who had since died. His objective was to obtain loans on his "property" so that he could buy an estate with real live serfs on it. One reason advanced for Equity's maneuvers was that it wanted to create sufficient profits to boost the price of its stock enough to enable it to buy a legitimate life insurance company and then "go straight." A simpler explanation is human greed, but if we accept Equity's aspirations as the "truth" it points to an admonition: that a company's profit-and-loss sheet is no more reliable than any other unverified fictional point of view.

An audited balance sheet for Equity as of April 1973, when it was forced into bankruptcy proceedings, showed scheduled liabilities exceeding assets by more than $42 million. At this time also, the company was preparing its 1972 annual report indicating assets of almost $750 million, earnings of over $22 million and stockholders' equity of more than $143 million.

This lighthearted bit of fiction was unfortunately never published. It would have provided a salutary lesson in how easily people can be duped.

Moral: Even a stopped clock is correct two times a day.

After Success, What?

Many successful people reach a certain plateau and stop there because they do not want to take further risks. This may make the remainder of their lives secure, but their obituaries will be dull and brief. They forget that success is mainly in the doing rather than the achieving. No man can accurately predict what the future will hold for him, yet goals can be set and each step can be prepared for. Huey Long, for example, before he reached the age of 20 had decided he would first hold a minor state office and would then become Governor of Louisiana, U.S. Senator, and finally President. He achieved three of these goals and was causing President Franklin D. Roosevelt much concern over the next election when he was assassinated in 1935. His maneuvers in preparing to win the Presidency had a decided influence on United States history. Long is often credited with driving Roosevelt to the left in the early days of the New Deal. By most criteria, he had a short but successful life. He accomplished what he had set out to do up to the point at which fate intervened, and in the process he affected the lives of millions of people, in a manner he considered beneficial.

Sometimes successful people have the opposite problem: their lives are long and their early successes so spectacular that they are their own "tough acts to follow." Alexander Graham Bell (who invented the telephone while still in his 20's) and Albert Einstein (his *General Theory of Relativity* was published when he was 36) are cases in point. Their solution was to "shift levels"—to enlarge the areas of their involvement. They no longer considered a mechanism or a theory as a goal (that had been accomplished), but rather all of the world itself as the goal, with constantly new challenges to be met with innovative actions.

Dealing with Successful People

"Hazard not your wealth on a poor man's advice" is an old saying that might be rephrased: "Deal with successful people." Successful people and those who want to be successful prefer to follow this rule in seeking advice. Usually they measure success in terms of wealth, power, or both. Other qualities a person may possess are ignored or downgraded with variations of that perennial question, "If you're so smart, why aren't you rich?"

Certainly there is some validity in using success as part of the measuring stick for the value of the advice that is given us. Successful people have probably encountered and overcome many problems that might seem insurmountable to us. They have learned techniques that work. They tend to apply these techniques to similar problems, and knowledge of them may be valuable to you.

If you are rich, there are assumptions that must be watched for. One is that people seek your counsel because you know the right way. Probably you did when you confronted particular problems that you successfully solved, but this was a day-by-day process, not one grand decision that "changed the world." Yet it is a constant temptation to the successful to reveal the "Ten Easy Steps" that led them to their present position. Even worse, they may in time begin to believe that their oversimplifications actually describe what happened. Consider how often the type of advice successful people give is not the type that they utilize for themselves. They try to entertain (How I got my first million) rather than enlighten (How I'm going to get my tenth). The first is history, the second, potentiality.

Humorist Art Buchwald criticizes a "successful" organization in noting that the Mafia advises that it is "lily-white and open only to males of Italian extraction." He continues:

> The Mafia has maintained that they could not run their enterprises except with Italian help. This is a 19th Century idea which has been passed down to the present Mafia families. . . . They are keeping out people who are well qualified, if not better, to do anything that a member of the Cosa Nostra could do. . . . You don't even need a college education to do most of the jobs that the Mafia requires of its members. . . . By opening the Mafia [they] would get fresh ideas, inspired leadership and youthful vigor that the organization so badly needs.

The Mafia's position could be compared to samples of advice that is advanced every day by successful men. Much of it is hackneyed, and very little is of the stunning originality of Buchwald's suggestion: "Why does a godfather always have to be head of a Mafia family? What would be wrong with having a godmother?"

You Have to Run Twice as Fast to Stay in the Same Place

Many harsh things have been said about the Bourbon kings who ruled in France after the abdication of Napoleon I. Napoleon himself called them "a set of imbeciles." Even more damning was Talleyrand's observation: "They have learned nothing and forgotten nothing." We have all encountered such people. When they are credited with a certain degree of accomplishment in a field, they fondly imagine that their status quo will always continue. Yet any realist recognizes that life moves on and requires us to improve, to develop, and to change. Probably very few professionals who have been out of school for ten years or more could pass the examination required of today's graduates. It is estimated that scientific information doubles every five years and knowledge in the other disciplines increases at about the same breakneck speed.

What is the established person to do? First of all, heed Satchel Paige's advice: "Don't look back. Something may be gaining on you." Let us be aware that time alone permits some younger persons to come up from behind. This can stimulate you to continually acquire new knowledge to match their speed. And remember, you can have the lead in experience. So much energy is wasted by people who have achieved some success but who, instead of continuing to grow, fight a rearguard action to prevent others from achieving equal goals. They have won and they want the game to be declared at an end. Since life is not a game, this is hardly possible. Life, however, does provide us with a challenge: to apply knowledge constantly to old problems. It would appear that basic human problems of life do not really change. What does change are the methods for dealing with them. Each age has its own tentative answers to these problems, just as each individual does. A hundred or more years ago, a word was coined to describe a successful man: millionaire. A person with $999,999 was "well-to-do" or "comfortably off," but he needed that extra dollar to be transformed into a special being, a millionaire. Once that magic plateau was reached, that was it. No one was ever spoken of as a "five-millionaire." "Multimillionaire" was sometimes used, although it did not add much glamour to the original word. Partly because a million today is a pathetic fragment of what it was 100 years ago and partly because so many more individuals qualify today, "millionaire" is no longer the popular descriptive word it once was. What one does and continues to do *are* important and descriptive. You can test this assertion by listing all of the important facts you know about George Washington. Is "the richest man in Colonial America" among them? Probably not. He had reached that status before he became general, first President, and Father of His Country. His wealth is just an irrelevant fact. His accomplishments after the fact are all-important.

So far we have stressed the opinion successful people have of themselves. What about the opinion of others? Well, it's not too promising. Public opinion polls have shown that where 60 to 80 percent of Americans used to consider politicians, religious leaders, educators, union leaders, lawyers, and many others basically good or worthy of respect, now only 10 to 25 percent do so. Clearly, this drop in confidence should be of concern to all of us. Not only do we have to run hard to keep up with ever-multiplying information; we run twice as fast to regain our self-regard.

Success Can Kill You

When Pyrrhus, King of Epirus, won a victory over the Romans at the Battle of Asculum in 279 B.C., his losses were so heavy that he exclaimed, "Another such victory and we are undone." Success in many fields can result in a pyrrhic victory. A small, intimate restaurant may suddenly become an "in" place. Then it is faced with the decision: expand and take advantage of potential new business or stay with the present situation. Either choice may be inappropriate. A larger restaurant may destroy the intimacy that drew the crowd in the first place. But by relying too much on the "in" group, the owner may become overconfident and relax standards—failure to follow through is the danger here—and a new restaurant will be "discovered." The "in" crowd is not known for its loyalty.

Many people have worked long and hard to build up a business, have seen it prosper and attract the attention of larger corporations or conglomerates. Should they sell? Often it depends on what they value: a generous price or the continuing status and satisfaction that the business has brought. Most people faced with this choice try to get both, and they may succeed. Public relations releases are full of such announcements as "Mr. Smith will remain as chief executive officer." But will he? Even with the best will in the world, both sides are binding themselves not to a business deal but to something more like marriage. How do they know they will be compatible as time goes by? Can they really work together each and every day? Quite often the answer is "No." The spectacular departure of Norman Cousins from *Saturday Review* in the 1970's, when the new owners came up with editorial ideas that Cousins could not force them to change, points to the dangers involved in this kind of deal. Later Cousins' opinion seemed to be vindicated when *Saturday Review* failed in its new form, but no one could derive any satisfaction from that.

Sometimes success does not bring satisfaction and carries within it the seeds of its own destruction. Often the people involved are not interested in creating a stable situation that can satisfy their creative needs. They are trophy collectors or compulsive shoppers. Without any appreciation, they buy paintings, chapels, castles—anything and everything that might come under the broad heading of art. Often they may never be uncrated. Mere acquisition was enough.

The New York Times ran this item:

> Roy C. Satchel has resigned as president of the Jos. Schlitz Brewing Company, effective April 1 [1973] after only six weeks in the post. He said in a statement issued by the company that his reasons were "wholly personal."
>
> . . . Reached at his home—he has already cleared out his desk at Schlitz—Mr. Satchel said that he just felt that the job was not for him. He added: "It was like climbing a mountain. Once you climbed it, you looked for another one to climb.
>
> . . . "I know it's hard for anyone to believe, but it's a very simple story. Everybody needs a certain kind of challenge. I need new goals, new enthusiasms, new challenges."
>
> . . . The post paid Mr. Satchel $160,000 a year. He owns 24,000 shares of Schlitz. If he had stayed until August 1, he would have been eligible to purchase 6,000 more shares at $20 each.

Moral: Fortune can become misfortune because of a slight miss.

Increasing the Success Probability

A district attorney recently dismissed a charge against him of improper campaign financing by airily quoting, *"De minimis lex non curat*—the law does not concern itself with trifles." The problem here is that what one man may consider a trifle can supply an important campaign issue to his opponent. A purposeful person rarely regards any relevant piece of information or possible alternative mode of action as too trivial to be considered to some degree. It can be important to try every door to be sure you have not passed up one leading to success.

In life situations involving other people, the only predictable outcome is likely to be that the unexpected will happen. However, to be prepared for the unexpected, one must first be prepared for the expected—prepared so that when the unexpected does happen, it can be met in an apt and innovative way. The doctrinaire who begins, "I'll tell you the *only* thing we're gonna do" is little prepared for opposition, let alone alternative solutions.

Can you prepare for a challenging life situation? Take as an example a possible way to obtain capital when you have a worthwhile idea that you wish to develop. These are a few working considerations.

1. Back up your confidence in the idea with a few dollars, whatever you can risk. Build some assets into your idea before you go out asking others to contribute capital.

2. Choose an effective presentation—a reliable map to guide the potential investor in the way that you think will be beneficial to both of you. Try to show what you see. A diamond in the rough is far less brilliant and valuable than one that is cut and polished.

3. Anticipate as far as possible all questions the investor might ask. Ask yourself questions from many points of view. It will clarify and sharpen your own awareness of the idea.

4. Reduce abstract ideas to concrete propositions in your presentation. "This will make us both a lot of money" is a worthless statement. Answers to such questions as How much profit for how much risk? What are the assumptions behind your facts? can have merit.

5. A written presentation can be very effective. Not only is it a straightforward approach, it tends to lessen the ambiguities that arise from an oral presentation. It can be one or a thousand pages, but be sure it is preceded by a summary sheet. State clearly in it how much capital is needed, when and how it is to be repaid, initial operating budget, and projected profits.

6. Try to have the investor look over your presentation while you are with him. Feedback is offered. Ambiguities can be cleared up and questions answered before they can create any doubts. This adds much to the written presentation.

7. Ask for enough money. Don't try to minimize start-up costs and other expenses in the hope of offering a "bargain." Investors are as cautious about bargains as any intelligent consumer.
8. Finally, don't try to shop a deal. Have a person who is knowledgeable put you in the presence of a person who is able to take your deal and might possibly like it. Spreading your force can weaken it.

Even if these considerations make a great deal of sense, they are not the *only* way. You must be open to change—even changing these suggestions. Sticking to absolute *rules* will diminish your success probability.

II
Failure

What Might Be Done

Dr. John A. Wheeler of Princeton has warned that it seems inevitable that the universe will collapse and become a "black hole." This is a superdense object thought to be the end product of the collapse of a large star. So great is the inward pressure that the star ceases to exist as matter, yet its gravity is so strong that no light, nor anything else, can escape from it.

People who have experienced failure can sympathize, having been there. Many of those who fail can recount step by step what it was that caused the collapse of their dreams, and it is true that little or no light is shed in the recounting. This is because the exercise becomes a litany of mourning—a chanting of what should and should not have been done in the past rather than as assessment of what might be done in the future.

A Failure Can Provide Successful Advice

Just as success has its overachievers and underachievers, failure has those who could have done more and those who should have done less. The former typically have not done their homework. They have not thought out and planned every step that must be taken. The following is a typical example: With the advent of detection by camera as a result of The Bank Protection Act, bank robbers have found it to be a much better practice to go into states other than their own, where they are less likely to be known and apprehended. One such robber left the Middle West and went to California. He waited outside the bank until 9:45 A.M., pulled the mask over his face, and rushed the door, only to be bounced back into the hands of a bank guard. The bank had not yet opened. "Golly," said the potential robber, "the banks back home open at nine A.M."

Failures who should have done less also often end up in court and possibly in jail. They are failures not because they were caught but because they took a carefully thought-out and balanced situation and added some superfluous or capricious detail. The temptation to do so might be termed the gaudy syndrome. They have to add one detail too many. Once a clothing merchant sued a wrecking company, claiming his merchandise had been damaged by water the company had used to settle the dust in an adjoining building that was being demolished. After more than two years the case came to trial. The jury seemed favorably impressed with the merchant's story. Then the judge asked if he had saved any of the damaged goods. He had and would bring some to court the following day. At that time he held up some woebegone baby clothes and was outraged when the defendant's lawyer said they looked undamaged to him. "Here, Your Honor," he shouted, "feel them. They're still wet!"

Another example is the Los Angeles thief who, having stolen a wallet and removed the money from it, decided with a gesture of magnanimity to return only the wallet to its recent owner. He drove by his victim and tossed it out to him. Later, when the police arrived to arrest him at his home, the thief discovered that he had thrown the wrong wallet—his own with *his* ID and photograph. His belated application of the Golden Rule, "Do unto others as you would have them do unto you," worked as promised. His lost wallet was also returned to him, but only after quite a few unpleasant legal formalities.

Achieving success is an art. Failures can be examples not of stupidity but of "bad" art. However, in today's world taste changes rapidly. What was "bad" yesterday sometimes becomes the trend tomorrow. Our assumptions often impel us to reject an idea whose time has come.

"Get a horse" was a cry that may have encouraged buggy-whip man-
ufacturers early in the century, but it assumed that things could not
be improved. "Four more years," no matter what your political persuasion, assumes the impossible, that the person in office can keep
delivering yearly the same administration like so many units of cloth—
all of one width, breadth, strength, and quality.

Since failures far outweigh successes in this world, how can we
profit from our own mistakes and the mistakes of others? First, a study
of failures can help us chart a course more accurately than success
can. Today's brilliant success may be no more than another pizza par-
lor tomorrow. At least failure tells us where not to go—if it is viewed
in the context of a particular time and place. Change the date and
circumstances, and a failure becomes a success. In the 1900's a young
couple bought a farm in southern Illinois but soon sold it because no
matter where they drilled, the well water "tasted of kerosene." This
was long before anyone thought of the area as having a potential for
producing oil. As we say: tastes change.

Sometimes Your Mistakes are Enough

Recently a columnist recalled a 19th-century British politician who
was "notorious all his life for clumsiness." His last act, when bowing
to the Prince of Wales, was to let himself be run over by a train which
was going 12 miles an hour. Probably he was waiting for the advice of
a protocol expert on when to rise. Many failures lack the confidence
to make their own mistakes. They must surround themselves with
partners, associates, experts so that they can share the blame. (People
who feel successful do not have this problem. No one wants to divide
up success.) Partners and associates can be very valuable in furthering
the success of a venture, but the hidden assumption that they can be
turned into scapegoats should the need arise can be a fatal one. The
assumption becomes a self-fulfilling prophecy. Then, too, no one should
be so naive as to think that associates will not have their own interests
at heart. They may have mutual interests, but their motivations are
probably quite different. Many have sworn undying loyalty to a superior and later turned state's evidence to save their own necks.

In searching for success, it is better if the responsibility is yours, the money is yours, and you are the person who signs the checks. You should listen to advice and evaluate it carefully. But your decision should be based entirely on your own judgments. Some people use this principle as their guiding light: they will not go into a business they cannot control, so that it will be only their own mistakes, if anything, that causes a failure.

Using Weakness as a Foundation for Strength

At a drinking party in Yugoslavia things got out of hand and a man bit off his best friend's ear. Later he tearfully apologized in public and begged for forgiveness. The friend refused: "I can't. You made me ugly." At that the first man whipped out a knife and slashed off one of his own ears. The two men are friends again.

This story demonstrates that who does what to whom is a vital element in most personal relationships. It also illustrates the deep-rooted instinct in many people to fight to overcome adversity and disparage the "quitter." We admire leaders who accept complete responsibility for the acts of their subordinates—John F. Kennedy and the Bay of Pigs fiasco comes to mind—versus leaders who claim all credit for successful acts and plead ignorance of things that have gone wrong. The first gain strength from what could have been a fatal weakness. The second create doubt and suspicion all about them.

Accomplished people make mistakes, of course, but they differ from others in knowing how to profit from them. Some of us may be familiar with the accidents that helped to produce the vulcanization of rubber or the use of penicillin in medicine. What is less often recognized is that while the "cause" of the discovery may be an accident, the positive application itself is the result of meticulous and careful preparation that changes "I did a dumb thing" to the ability to cry "Eureka!"

The May 1986 edition of *Scientific American* had an article on the cheetah:

> . . . a virtual running machine [and] model of aerodynamic engineering. Its skull is lightweight and its limbs are long and slender, not unlike

a greyhound's. Its heart, vascular system, lungs and adrenal glands are all enlarged, enhancing the animal's ability to accelerate and navigate during a high-speed chase. . . .

These various adaptations have made the cheetah a particularly effective hunter on the flat, open savannas of central and southern Africa, where it has a higher rate of successful kills than even the lion. After stalking its prey the cheetah launches a high-speed chase (often clocked at up to 70 miles per hour), pushes over or trips its winded victim and swiftly kills the prey by strangulation in its strong feline jaws. . . .

However, the cheetah is threatened with extinction.

As a result of intensive inbreeding generations ago, each cheetah appears to be nearly identical. . . .

When a species has little genetic variety, its ranks are unlikely to contain many members whose genetically determined traits are well suited to withstand ecological change; the species competes poorly for survival under changed conditions and may die out.

Moral: As Robert Browning said: "What comes to perfection perishes." An occasional failure enhances the self-advice process.

On the other hand, there are also people who go through life vainly boasting of and acting on their weaknesses as though they were strengths. Examples of this misdirected energy are libertines, alcoholics, people who "say what they think," whatever the consequences. Like Peter Pan, they proclaim by their acts, "I won't grow up." There is nothing wrong with sex, liquor, or frankness, but should they dominate a person's life to the exclusion of other worthwhile pursuits, other alternatives?

Three men went into a restaurant for lunch. When the waiter came to take their order, one said he had been very much upset the last time he had been in because he had been given soup in a dirty bowl. The waiter apologized and assured him it would never happen again. All three thereupon ordered soup. When the waiter returned with a loaded tray, he asked, "Who was the one who ordered the clean bowl?"

Moral: As infants we start dealing with life from a position of weakness. If we try hard and often enough, we are able to knock down all the pins for a strike; some of us even end up with a clean soup bowl.

The Uncertainty of Power and Timing

Most people who believe that for every "winner" in a life negotiation there must be a "loser" also tend to believe they must have absolute power in order to win. A strong position in a negotiation is very comforting. Many, however, do not realize where their true strength lies: they underestimate or overestimate it and, because they do not understand it, often misapply it. In human intercourse, power cannot be viewed as brute strength that bludgeons "enemies" to their knees. No one "wins" in that kind of situation.

Power is a historical label that we use to explain why things have happened in the past. As events occur, no one can predict who will be powerful and who will be defeated.

In an international example, this was apparent time and time again throughout the United States' participation in the Vietnam War. Although immeasurably more powerful than North Vietnam, no matter what military or political tactics, short of nuclear weapons, it tried, the United States could never impose its will on the North Vietnamese. Even the most intense bombing in the history of the world brought only a tenuous cease-fire that was more often violated than observed. The North Vietnamese merely stood fast and waited. They used a strategy of forbearance.

Time is an element of strength, but often we do not know how to utilize it. Of the observation "This, too, shall pass away," Abraham Lincoln said, "How chastening in the hour of pride! How consoling in the depths of affliction!" Time works changes in our affairs and circumstances, not only in important matters, but in the small ones as well. There is not a single detail of our lives that is not affected by time. Some aspects, like the aging process, cannot be notably altered by any decision we may make. However, the way we view the process and how we cope with the problems that arise can definitely alter the quality and strength of our lives. Too many people decide early in life that retirement is the " only" answer to the problem of aging. They place an artificial time limit on their business careers, sometimes only to find that the same limit applies to their life span as well.

The distortions that are created by trying to establish limits and thus stop time itself can be seen in a pristine state in the behavior of

American politicians. If they themselves do not impose the time limit, their terms in office do. In the United States of America the term is usually set at two, four, or six years. Seldom can politicians be sure they will be reelected, so they are caged in by their terms. In the first half of the term they will take care of the things they feel may outrage the voters; the second half is spent trying to placate them. Taxes are usually raised at the beginning of a legislative session and lowered before election day. Special interests are accommodated in the beginning and castigated at the end.

Failure to consider time limits adequately also distorts the decision-making process. A rather sad item in the newspaper reported the closing of a turkey-feather-duster factory. Operated by a single family for 102 years, the company was forced out of business by rising costs and competition from aerosols and vacuum cleaner attachments. Four generations, from the inventor of the turkey-feather duster in 1872 to his great-granddaughter who closed the factory, were involved. The latter explained: "I ran the company the last few years and, well, you see, well, I guess maybe I didn't do a very good job. Or something happened."

Yet 23 years before, her brother, Mr. Hoag, was quoted in the local newspaper as saying: "As long as there is dust, there will be a demand for feather dusters. And as long as there is a Hoag and a turkey with feathers, the Hoag Duster Company will continue to do business."

We all wish it were true, but we should know better.

It seems to be a human trait to impose deadlines on oneself ("I'm going to be a millionaire by the time I'm 30") or on others ("You have to do this in 48 hours"). Even Communist leaders who do not have to please the voters have their five-year plans. Perhaps the only ones who can objectively use the flow of time to envision strategies and tactics that extend far into the future are corporation executives and bureaucrats. Yet we are all well aware that they, too, are tied into their office-holding periods.

For a case in point involving strength and timing, one should remember when the all-powerful General Motors took on Ralph Nader. At that time Nader was a young, not yet experienced lawyer who had written a book, *Unsafe at Any Speed,* which severely criticized the automobile manufacturer. Rather than freshly examining their position and the future potential effect on car buyers, General Motors executives decided to eliminate Nader as they would swat a fly. Someone said, "Do something. Do anything. But do it now!" The impulsive response was to put detectives on Nader's trail on the assumption—in this case false—that "everyone has something to hide." The results were disastrous for them.

Within every large company, policies and objectives must be related to the "here and now" existing world. Often there is nothing wrong with a corporate objective of concentrating completely on the economic aspects of doing business. However, the other objectives, such as social, political, health, and environmental objectives, should not be ignored. No alert management would try to sweep these concerns aside. In time, favorable public opinion may be of more importance to the corporation than its net profits for the year. The protective legislation and millions of cars that have been recalled since Nader began his crusade should point to that fact. Time is sometimes a factor of strength.

As corporations have grown powerful and profitable, they have also developed hidden weaknesses masking as strengths labeled "new and improved." There once was a time B.C. (before computers) when no one could honestly challenge their telephone company's monthly statement. Today it is amazing how our phone bills show a circle of friends and clients that has expanded to places we have never heard of and numbers we have never called. Of course, today's bank statements, also subject to computeritis, are no longer a model of accuracy either. But banks have succeeded in some ways in keeping abreast of the times and making money in still another manner. Who in the United States would have thought a few decades ago that banks could transform that cardinal sin, the bounced check, into a shining virtue, the instant bank loan?

Moral: Time, in passing, changes strength to weakness and weakness to strength.

III
Motivation

Achieving through Motivation

A West Virginian was charged with littering because he "willfully and unlawfully placed, deposited, dumped and threw. . . . into the Ohio River the carcass of a dead animal, to wit, the dead body of one Rocco Wayne Thompson." The accused had earlier won acquittal on a charge of murdering Mr. Thompson by pleading self-defense. Like some prosecuting attorneys, we classify and ascribe to others many motivations that are not even proved in a court of law. Then, in a fit of frustration, if the outcome is not satisfactory we bend facts to fit our preconceptions. Disposing of the body of a murder victim becomes littering. Thus we pervert one of the most positive concepts, motivation, into a weapon of self-justification and revenge. Motivation of ourselves and others deserves better than this. It is one of the most powerful tools that we can learn to use in achieving success. And all we need do is observe ourselves and others carefully and dispassionately—not to manipulate life but to utilize the leverage that permits us to shift situations from "win/lose" to "everybody wins."

Don't Let Them Push Your Buttons

While walking with a friend, a minister stopped at a newstand to buy a newspaper. The transaction was a long and unpleasant one because the minister did not have change and the news dealer was determined to be as uncivil as possible. After it was finally over, the minister calmly turned and walked on. When the friend asked, "How can you possibly deal with a person like that?" the minister replied, "I don't let him push my buttons."

It is very difficult to be always in control of oneself. We are more likely to respond to outer stimuli than to inner direction. In our daily bouts with the world, we meet so many potential sources of exasperation—from train conductors to bank presidents—that if we respond negatively, we are placed at the mercy of the world, not in control of ourselves. A prime example is the driver having to cope with heavy traffic conditions. One hour in the average car generates more frustration and anger than one could encounter in a week of melodramas.

What is a primary cause of button-pushing? At the risk of sounding old-fashioned, it is a lack of courtesy on the part of others. We all feel we are entitled to a degree of respect, although some of us will not take the time to avoid situations that might embarrass others. Bill Hosokawa, an associate editor of *The Denver Post,* told this story:

> Not long ago I was introduced at a cocktail party to a fairly important political figure. Noticing my Japanese features and trying to make conversation, he asked, "Mr. Hosokawa, how long have you been in our country?"
>
> If I had spoken with an accent the question would have been logical, but I am American-born and American-educated and make my living as a writer and editor in English.
>
> Noting his youth, I replied with a smile: "Sir, I think I have been in our country ten or fifteen years longer than you."
>
> He blushed as he realized his faux pas. "I'm sorry," he said. "I just wasn't thinking."

Most of us are not intentionally rude. Rather, like the politician, we are thoughtless. Intentionally rude people are usually avoided or treated like the "characters" they are. They can and should do little to raise our blood pressure. However, it is easy to sympathize with those who because of economic pressures have to deal on a regular basis with such people.

All too often we ourselves can be the cause of such rudeness in our relationships. Although we like to think of ourselves as calm, reasonable, and unfailingly courteous, we become thoughtless, or "It's one of those days." Unless we are fortunate enough to recall the person whose buttons can't be pushed, we enter into a vortex of negatively oriented emotions. Nothing seems to be able to stop our descent except exhaustion. Certainly, no one profits from it.

How can we prevent the situation from ever arising? Chiefly by self-control. So many of us think of "our rights" as God-given while those of others are granted only by our tolerance. It should be the other way around: we should earn the acceptance by others of our rights and we should grant them the right to judge us according to our merits. This should be basic even to any advice that we give ourselves. As Edmund Burke said: "It is not what a lawyer tells me I *may* do, but what humanity, reason, and justice tell me I ought to do."

Motivate Without Money

"Is it true," an auto worker asked wistfully, "that you get to do fifteen different jobs on a Cadillac?" "I heard," said another, "that with Volvos you follow one car all the way down the line."

Such are the yearnings of young auto workers at the Vega plant in Lordstown, Ohio. Their average age is twenty-four, and they work on the fastest auto assembly line in the world. Their jobs are so subdivided that few workers can feel they are making a car.

—Barbara Garson in
"Luddites in Lordstown"

It is easy to say that "Money will buy anything but poverty." This, however, is a superficial attempt at analyzing the basic motivation of human beings. While it is true that money will enable us to buy what we want most of the time, it cannot in and of itself change people's attitudes. And this in turn affects how people do their jobs. Although it is popular today to deplore the shoddiness of practically everything, we tend to forget that pride of craftsmanship has always commanded a premium price and fine products can still be found today if you are willing to pay the price. But it should be noted that money here is not the initial motivating factor. Demand for superior goods, however, is the factor that makes prices high, and the superior goods are produced by well-motivated workers.

It is well to remember as employer that if employees depend on you only for money, you will probably lose them (if they are any good at all) to a higher bidder. A partial exception to the rule, because of exclusion from antitrust laws, could be found in the dealings of owners of professional baseball teams. Red Smith wrote: "Far more typical [of their lack of awareness and foresight] is the blind obstinacy they showed during the recent strike, when they voted in advance to reject all offers and thus tied the hands of their 'negotiator' . . . even before he went into bargaining sessions." In other words, they would not budge. The status quo would be preserved. The only motivation this provided the players was to hate the owners and beat them at any cost. Red Smith further said of the owners: "If they are sometimes less than sensitive in their dealings with the help, it's probably because they have grown so accustomed to regarding the players as possessions that they forget the players are people. Their speech betrays this. 'The strongest arm in the league,' they say of this man, or 'a great pair of hands. . . .' "

People demand a greater satisfaction than being regarded as property. Slave revolts, violent labor strikes, and other popular upheavals throughout history confirm that people are motivated not by money alone but at least partially by a desire for that vague abstraction, "a better life." Sometimes this can mean a very small change, but nonetheless a change. In 1927, the Western Electric Company's Hawthorne plant, in Illinois, experimented to determine the effect of "better" incentives on workers' production. The executives were delighted at first to find that when incentives increased, so did production. But to their dismay, when these were decreased production still went up. In what was later termed the "Hawthorne effect," the experimenters discovered that "better" incentives did not solely motivate the workers. What apparently happened was that by participating in a worthwhile experiment they were given a feeling of self-esteem and therefore worked better.

Moral: People do not resist change; they resist being changed.

Even Death Can Motivate

When I was invited by the Northwest Territorial Government of Canada to present The Art of Negotiating Seminar® to its employees, I got an insight into what motivates people that I had never had before. Many of the workers, I noticed, were Eskimos. (An English word. They prefer their own word, Innuit, "the people.") After the seminar, I was socializing with them over a few drinks. We got along so well that I asked a rather flippant question: "Aren't you the fellows who throw your old grandmothers out in the snow to freeze to death?" Good-humoredly and without hesitation, one replied: "Jerry, we *never* throw our grandmothers out in the snow. They *ask* to go."

Having been put down, ever so gently, I did my homework. I found that the family is the most important unit in Innuit life. Everyone is involved in a fight for survival. The men hunt or work, the women perform the domestic tasks, the old men mend tools and weapons, while the grandmothers care for children and chew the tough hides used for clothing until they are pliable. The children are loved, but they are expected to learn proper behavior and their roles as adults from the example of their elders.

The grandmothers ask to be put out in the snow because they can no longer contribute to the welfare of the family. They have one consolation, however. Although, for the first five days after death, a soul is considered evil and harmful, on the sixth day, they believe, the soul is inherited by a newborn child, who is given its name. This acceptance of death as a final, natural rite of passage that preserves the dead person's memory is somehow more civilized than the "warehousing" of our elders in nursing homes, "unwept, unhonored and unsung."

What You Don't Know *Can* Hurt You

Sayings such as "Ignorance is bliss" and "What you don't know won't hurt you" seem at first consideration to be based on precedents: Eve and the Tree of Knowledge; Prometheus giving fire to mankind and receiving horrible punishment; Oedipus doggedly pressing for facts that will prove him the murderer of his father. But when life permits a choice, consider that knowledge is power and worthy of the quest. For some, however, the search for knowledge proves too strenuous. As a consequence, they rationalize and give up the quest by denigrating the goal.

Many religious fabrics have had anti-intellectual threads running through them. Still, there have always been men—Socrates and Galileo, to mention two—who have advanced their search for truth to the limit regardless of the sectarian consequences. Further reconsideration of the precedents reveals that man *did* learn; man *was* given the use of fire by Prometheus; Thebes *was* freed of the plague as a result of Oedipus' discovery; and Socrates and Galileo *did* gain an immortality that few human beings attain.

To be motivated by the pure and simple desire for knowledge is not confined to a few giants in history. A. H. Maslow says, "The enjoyment of puzzles and problems is a *primate* characteristic, not just human." He cites the case of a monkey in a completely walled-in cage who performed complex actions for the sole pleasure of looking through a window for a few seconds. This has a reverberation in the strike of General Motors workers in a high-speed Vega assembly plant, not over money but over the utterly meaningless, repetitive motions they had to go through day after day. Their boredom and frustration may have been mirrored in massive 1972 recalls of Vegas because of possible fire hazards involving fuel and exhaust systems.

The mentally healthy person has a curiosity, a desire for purposeful activity, and a need to know and understand. The neurotic is often marked by a fear of learning anything new, a desire to preserve the status quo—which might be defined as holding on to what you have rather than getting what you want.

While most people want to know the "truth," people wishing to be successful in business are required to seek it. Often this can be difficult. They are mainly dependent on subordinates for firsthand information. However, ambitious executives have their own little empires to protect. They naturally want to "look good," and their combined reports to the boss can present a rosy picture so far from reality as to be nothing but reckless fantasy. One sees such examples every day in newspaper reports on government operations, at both local and national levels. The perceptive businessperson must ferret out facts in his or her own organization by probing and questioning every so-called "report" encountered. No determining "fact" should be accepted until you and the bearer of it agree on its operations and have considered the sources and assumptions upon which the fact is based. The great Howard Hughes "autobiography" fraud offers a constructive example and a moral: Clifford Irving returned to New York from the island of Ibiza confident that he could talk his way out of the charges that were being leveled against him. However, after a particularly trying interview with the district attorney, he returned to his lawyer's home, where he was staying. There he was confronted with an oral message from two reporters that they knew "all about Meier." Irving's confident air collapsed. He hurried back to the district attorney and confessed the outline of the conspiracy. Later he found that Meier (an innocent bystander) was not the Meyer he had thought it was. Some people are convinced when they hear it; some when they write it; others when they see it in writing; too few go beyond the words.

There are many different reasons why the truth is sometimes withheld from us. *Kennedy Justice,* by Victor S. Navasky, tells of a two-day meeting between representatives of the Attorney General's office and the FBI in which the former thought the FBI had agreed to publish testimony of Joseph Valachi on La Cosa Nostra. Later, the FBI protested that the decision had been made against its will. As one Justice Department spokesman said: "We made the mistake of dealing with them like we did with everybody else. You talked something out, reached a decision and carried it out. We didn't understand that they never really said what they were thinking." Of course, another explanation is that sometimes we hear only what we want to hear.

Whatever the motivations people may have for concealing the truth, we must still seek it. As Maslow says, "The old saw 'What you don't know won't hurt you' turns out to be false at a deeper level. Just the contrary is true. It is just what you don't know that *will* hurt you. What you don't know has power over you; knowing it brings it under your control and makes it subject to your choice. Ignorance makes real choice impossible."

Getting a Second Mental Wind

William James in "The Energies of Men" comments on a familiar phenomenon:

> On usual occasions we make a practice of stopping an occupation as soon as we meet the first effective layer . . . of fatigue, have then walked, played, or worked "enough," so we desist. That amount of fatigue is an efficacious obstruction on this side of which our usual life is cast. But if an unusual necessity forces us to press onward, a surprising thing occurs. The fatigue gets worse up to a certain critical point, when gradually or suddenly it passes away, and we are fresher than before. We have evidently tapped a level of new energy, masked until then by a fatigue-obstacle usually obeyed. There may be layer after layer of this experience.

We have all experienced this phenomenon; yet, strangely, although the ultimate feeling we have on getting a second wind is a profound satisfaction, we are not likely to push for it unless compelled to by external forces. If left on our own we tend to behave like a rat in a maze—drawn by hunger toward food, yet driven away from it by fear of an electric shock. So we travel up and down the maze, alternately attracted and repelled, achieving a middle ground of mediocrity.

Those who consciously strive to attain a second mental wind often resort to a kind of stop-start driving, moving from crisis to crisis. Although the stimulus is self-induced, the pressure still comes from outside and is not subject to any control except the ability to call the whole thing off. There is a better way: to set goals that are desirable enough to overcome inertia and fear and also lift us until we get a second mental wind. Thus the results are more likely to be predictable and positive than the results that would ensue if we were merely driven to them.

Gresham's Law, which states that bad money tends to drive out good because people hoard the good money and spend the bad, often operates on the human achievement level as well. We tend to hoard our creative time and spend lavishly the time we devote to routine tasks. We do not realize that although we might spend more creative time than we do, untapped reserves still remain, as do the possibilities of a second, third, and even fourth mental wind. Where we make our mistake is in regarding each plateau of creativity we reach as the highest level we can possibly attain. There we settle down, build a house, and prepare to spend the remainder of our lives. Instead, we should constantly reevaluate our goals, discarding or upgrading those we have already achieved (or relegating them to the routine tasks they have actually become). Our goals should always be on a higher level (not "This is the way we have always handled this problem," but "How can I achieve a goal that I have never reached before?").

Few of us would consider abandoning a successful career in the middle of our lives to try a new career that has no connection with our previous training. However, Albert Schweitzer did this when he left a notable career as musicologist and organist to study medicine and ultimately become a medical missionary. He was forced to make an either/or choice, since time and location dictated it. (A primitive outpost in Africa and a career in classical music are hardly compatible.) But most of us do not need to make an either/or choice. We can expand our career or add new ones. We can accept our achievements as ultimate goals or as stepping-stones to new ones — all this by imaginatively using the concept of a second wind. There is no cost involved. We are using energies we already possess but have not fully utilized.

Which Goal Is "Best"?

When you are a child, it is very easy to answer the question, "What do you want to be when you grow up?" An enthusiasm of the moment provides the answer: a fireman, a football player, a clown. These aspirations rarely last the year, and adolescence is almost sure to put an end to them. After a period of self-doubt, some of us emerge in our late teens or early 20's with a clear idea of what we want to do with our lives and take steps to prepare for a career. After that there is a reliance on sheer luck, "pull," or dogged determination to carry us over an imaginary goal line. There we stop, having "won the game."

If, however, we are not hung up on a game analogy but rather consider life as a perpetual challenge to the potentialities that lie within us, we do not stop at any point. We constantly seek new goals that will keep us alive and alert long after others have retired to their rocking chairs.

In seeking goals, some people are horizon-bound. They cannot conceive of any goal that lies outside the circumscribed world that they are familiar with. In earlier ages, of course, this was the customary way to attain wealth—by the slow and steady accumulation of land or by sending others out to gather wealth for the merchant prince. Today the sedentary life does not produce the satisfactions of wealth or sense of achievement that it once did. To achieve our goals we must move forward both mentally and physically.

But what goals should we aim for? There is really no limit. Preferably a goal should challenge us to new exertions. Often it will be found in the new frontiers of human thought that keep expanding day by day. Those of us who can look back 20 years can pick out any number of goals that we probably neglected. We might call this the "If only I had . . ." list. All of us can look back and see what we should have done. The difficult thing is to choose what we now should do. For most of us that might be to build on the foundations of what we already know, to stretch our knowledge to the limit, and see how we can go beyond that limit in a way that will be beneficial to ourselves and to others.

People are often inhibited from setting goals because they unconsciously assume that only the most grandiose schemes can succeed. They are bemused by the fact that a phenomenal success—Xerox, for example—is a giant now. They cannot conceive of its ever having been a concept and a goal—and nothing more.

Others believe that a goal, to be successful, must create "a whole new industry." This is fine if it can be done, but it isn't necessary. William Blake speaks of the ability "to see a world in a grain of sand." This can offer as satisfying and rewarding a goal as the most innovative grand idea. Robert H. Abplanalp, for example, became known as "the father of modern aerosols," a $3 billion business, not because he thought up the concept of the aerosol (he didn't) but because he made an aerosol valve "that really worked at a price no one could refuse."

Along the same line, many people think of Robert Fulton as the inventor of the first steamboat. He wasn't; John Fitch was. But Fulton invented the first *practical* steamboat.

Moral: Cost, effectiveness and other factors can be successful goals just as much as brand-new concepts.

IV
Time

Timeliness

W. C. Fields is said to have picked up a rosebud, looked at it intently and commanded, "Bloom, damn you, bloom!" Few of us have the patience to wait until a process has fully evolved, the gestation period has taken place, the metamorphosis has come into being. Time deals with change. A process and a situation in changing can ripen by degrees. In any relationship a consideration of the timing, as to when something is done and when something is said, can be most appropriate and most important. This holds true whether we move too soon or wait too long. All the following words deal with the same realization: development, appropriateness, proper timing, and timely. In the consideration of any act such terms should be taken into account. Development is not the same as change. Both, however, are contained in the process of time.

According to mythology, Rome was destined to be founded by men of Trojan blood. Aeneas was the leader of these men. At the fall of Troy, he was able to escape with the help of his mother, Venus. All was in turmoil as Troy fell, yet he brought out his little son and his father. His men, on seeing Aeneas carrying his father on his shoulders, asked in amazement why he had taken the risk to bring him out. To this he replied, "As we are destined to found a great city, we will need the aged knowledge that this man possesses."

Too many people today are prepared to discard past experience as not relevant. Neither the old nor the new is by itself sufficient. Man has struggled too long and hard to have his past experiences ignored. The future problems will be solved by techniques yet to be discovered, guided by the accumulated wisdom of human kind.

Moral: Your future is the solution of the problems of your past, when you have lived long enough to have learned from your experiences.

A Difference Can Make a Difference

Two Zen priests on a long journey met a group of women going to a wedding. They had stopped at a stream, afraid to cross because the water might ruin their beautiful gowns. One of the priests offered to carry them across and did so while the other priest scowled and watched. Then the priests continued on their way. After a while the second one said, "I saw what you did back there with those women. You have violated your vows." The first replied, "Are you still thinking about those women? I left them back at the stream." How we look at things depends in part on when we look at them.

The scientific method depends on the theory that any valid experiment can be duplicated and the same results will be obtained. Most scientists who firmly believe this also believe that nothing can be absolutely duplicated. They say there are many variables, among them time, that prevent perfect duplication. Yet this is not considered an inconsistency. What they are doing is viewing the world on different levels. On the macroscopic level the variables do not add up to significant difference. A good cook might tell you that you can cook an egg one day in a shorter time than on other days, even though temperature and other conditions under the cook's control remain the same. Or that gingersnaps won't "snap" if baked on a hot, humid day. These are simple examples of why cooking is regarded as an art, not a science.

John D. Rockefeller once said, "Good management consists of showing average people how to do the work of superior people." This is the kind of simplistic nonsense 19th-century captains of industry were fond of uttering. However, even Dr. Frankenstein did not have much success with that theory. We rather doubt that Rockefeller created thousands of little John D.'s to populate his corporate world, and he probably wouldn't have appreciated them if he had. It is a characteristic of some human beings to consider themselves unique, different from anyone else in the world, and there is justification in thinking so. Similarities among individuals in a society or a business must also be considered; otherwise there can be no communication between them, no common goal to be realized. Their similarities hold an organization together. Their differences enrich the association and prevent it from being turned into an army of robots ruled by, as Rockefeller implied, "superior people."

It is interesting to note that Rockefeller in his old age, after a lifetime devoted to showing other robber barons how to "really" do it, became depressed about his public image. He didn't want the difference to matter. How could he get people to stop hating him? Instead of believing his own cant, he did what most persons would do: he hired an expert who knew more about a particular field than he did. The expert's solution? Philanthropy. It worked. Within living memory, University of Chicago undergraduates could be heard singing, "Praise John, from whom oil blessings flow."

Moral: Time does make a difference.

Make Up My Mind for Me

A zipper company put out a billboard advertisement which read, "When you can bear the burdens of life, that is called strength." Underneath, someone wrote, "When you get others to bear it for you, that is called intelligence." This cynical viewpoint has a certain vogue today, and most of those who offer professional advice would probably say it has never been out of style. If you are inclined to accept it, consider the man who was killed in the collapse of a Greenwich Village hotel. Just before his death he was on the phone to the desk clerk complaining that the windows were falling out. Some of us are so accustomed to shifting our burdens onto others that when we are confronted with major problems, we don't know what to do. The decision-making process, like the body, can grow flabby through lack of exercise. And one of the most important decisions we have to make (but seldom do) is *when* to act. Instead we let circumstances make the decision for us. Or we act like robots at the command "You must act now!" Often the command is an invitation to participate in a con game. "Act now before you lose out" is implied. "Act now so I can make a fast getaway" is unfortunately the hidden meaning. In this case, with a quick decision we let time work against our best interests rather than for them. To the people who have been called by advertising copywriters the "Now" generation, an extended period of time is like a prison sentence—something to be avoided at all costs or endured grudgingly if necessary. Life to them is like a game of blackjack with time as the dealer. The decision is made quickly: "Hit me." No time is wasted in granting that request.

Time might best be regarded as flexible. Many of us would prefer fresh milk but aged cheddar, antique furniture but modern plumbing, ancient oaks but this year's flowers. Each has its merits, but the time necessary to produce them varies greatly.

Levi's, the tight-fitting denim pants, were first made up for California '49-ers. They were sturdy and long-wearing. They also earned their originator, Levi Strauss, and his successors a fortune. They still bring in a fortune, but some stores discovered they could get almost twice as much for well-worn Levi's as they could for brand-new ones. The company, in turn, found a laundry owner who could create instantly aged Levi's. (The process is said to be a secret, but we suspect it is merely the ancient lore of laundrymen everywhere.) Thus we have three different versions of a single basic product: new Levi's, well-worn Levi's, and stone-washed Levi's. Different amounts of time are used to produce them, and you alone make the choice as to which time best suits your purpose. For this you can apply seat-of-the-pants wisdom.

Moral: Time is a constant innovator.

Task/Time Get Work Done

Over the centuries, the dream of many mad scientists and even a few sane ones has been the perpetual-motion machine. This would be a mechanism so efficient that once started it would never stop running. Unfortunately, gravity, friction, and other abrasive forces act as much on machines as they do on human beings. Both are slowed down, but today if a machine were to operate at only 10 to 15 percent of potential, it would be considered inefficient. Yet that range is the average efficiency rating of human beings. No one factor accounts for this appalling waste of potential, but ranking high is our tendency to personify time—or Father Time, to give "him" the "proper" title. We say that time is against us or for us, there's not enough of it, it flies, it goes, it can be kept, we can catch up with it if we happen to lose a little. All these human characteristics we attribute to time. Implied in this is that time calls the shots and we are only its passive servant. To some degree this may, unfortunately, be true. We are forced to utilize time to satisfy our many physical needs—sleep, food, elimination, travel, and so forth. With the small portion of time that's left over we are often forced to consider what has been called the tyranny of the urgent.

Then where do we find the time to do what we want and need to do? First, it is important to realize that we unthinkingly tend to divide our days into short and long time segments: time to be alone, time to be in company, time for travel, and so on. When we become conscious of these types of time segments, we can arrange our tasks on the basis of time allocation. We can always have a number of tasks ready to be performed, and as the appropriate time segment appears, we should try to put the right task into that time slot. This concept I call task/time segments. Applying it can be true time-consciousness, because we view the tasks on the basis of the time allocation that is needed. We are therefore not attempting to manage time but merely to use it. To restate, it's merely doing a task when the appropriate time period becomes available for that task. As we grow more skilled in discovering these task/time segments, we will learn to combine and sandwich in many other tasks and functions and be able to do two or three things during the same period—not simultaneously in most cases, but during the same particular time segment. Some tasks can be combined with others in the same time segment. For example, the reading of a newspaper shows the potential of multiple use of time. As you read you mark, you clip, take notes, you put away for future reference. You cut out articles that you think friends or business associates might be interested in, to send to them in the mail. You learn more about their interests in that manner.

Try to finish the task in the time segment allocated. This is far less time-consuming than continually going back to finish. There are short-term tasks that can be immediately finished, but there are also long-term goals. These long-term goals can be arrived at by breaking the tasks into manageable sectional quantities. This permits better handling. Setting a realistic deadline based on personal experience can also be of assistance. You know yourself. You know whether you are going to feel like not doing something; allow also for surprises and emergencies. Utilizing these methodologies, we take a different point of view. Instead of managing Father Time, we manage those things which are within our control—namely, the tasks that we wish to accomplish.

Ready or Not, Here I Come

One hot summer day, 35 squealing and shouting Long Island children boarded a bus to go to Jones Beach. The driver took an unusual route—perhaps to avoid the beach traffic, observers thought—and parked in front of the Nassau County Court House. He got off the bus, leaving the children, and went inside, where he joined his lawyer in a courtroom. When the judge took his place on the bench, the driver asked for postponement of sentencing so that he could first drive the children to the beach. It seems he had been charged with grand larceny, but the charge was reduced to petty larceny when he agreed to plead guilty to the lesser charge. The judge looked stunned when he realized that both he and the children were expected to act as mere pawns in the driver's search for an "easy" solution to his problems with time.

He said, "This is incredible. I will not release you. I am going to send you to jail."

"It was my understanding, Your Honor," the driver replied, "that I was to receive probation for my plea."

In response to the new problem, the driver withdrew his plea of guilty. "In that case," the judge retorted, "I will restore the grand larceny charge. Trial set for September fourteenth."

Two hours after they had set out, the children were finally driven to the beach by a substitute driver. They were considerably more subdued and no doubt puzzled by the vagaries of adult behavior.

Although grand larceny will probably not be the charge lodged against us for our untimely actions, many of us are guilty of the same mental processes the driver used. We feel that when we are ready to do something and know where we want to do it, the world should be ready to accommodate our whims. As the driver discovered, this seldom happens. But we keep trying. Some young people, especially college graduates looking for their first permanent job, often fall victim to this attitude. When do they want to start looking for employment? "Maybe in the fall after I've had a good vacation." Where do they want to work? "Someplace where I can help people. I hear San Diego is nice. Anything out there where I could work part-time?" College placement counselors may tear their hair, but the business world is not affected by these attitudes. There the self-indulgent sink without a ripple. However, many of these emerge later, struggling to the surface. They are young enough and their attitudes flexible enough so that most eventually learn to accommodate themselves to the "reality" of the world at a particular moment.

Time Offered Weighty Evidence

Once people have obtained the "best" advice they can get, the tendency is to take it and run with it. Often the result is, "Marry'd in haste, we may repent at leisure." The reason often is that they have sought advice expecting to get a quick solution to a pressing problem. This point of view rarely works in our process world. There is no such thing as a "final solution" to any problem, although many murders are predicated on this belief.

The continuing ripple effect of advice is vividly illustrated in a horror story about a Baltimore doctor. In 1983, the doctor was accused of raping a 24-year-old woman who was babysitting with his daughter. Not surprisingly, the doctor rushed to find a lawyer. How he chose him was not reported, but the attorney offered an "easy" way out. The doctor should enter a so-called Alford plea, in which the defendant does not admit guilt but concedes the evidence could result in a conviction. In a plea bargain, the doctor got a suspended four-year sentence.

This seemed a happy ending to a serious problem. Only his reputation suffered a loss. However, the process did not stop there. The babysitter then filed a lawsuit seeking damages. The doctor's lawyer, who seemed to have an aversion to courtrooms, offered no defense, and the doctor was ordered to pay the woman $4 million.

Finally, the doctor looked within for his own advice. He might not have known about plea bargaining, but in this litigious age, *every* doctor knows about the uses and abuses of malpractice suits. He hired a new lawyer and brought suit against the first lawyer, easily winning a $7 million malpractice judgment. The judge at this trial said the first lawyer had "failed in every possible way," that his "performance is shockingly inadequate, far below any notion of an acceptable level of competence. If the court has ever seen an injustice rendered by the ineptitude of a lawyer, this is it."

Possibly the most telling detail of this story is that the doctor, almost as an afterthought during the second trial, recalled and testified that he weighed 140 pounds and the "raped babysitter" weighed in at 200 pounds. Instead of blindly following the advice of an incompetent attorney, he should have remembered another piece of good advice: "The show isn't over until the fat lady sings." Perhaps this, too, will happen. When last heard from, the doctor had appealed the $4 million award to a higher court. In our process world, he may even enlarge a $3 million profit into $7 million.

It should be noted that the events to this point took three years and show no sign of ending.

Moral: Use advice to start your thinking, not to end it.

V
Assumptions

Building Blocks of Ideas

Once upon a time, an Associated Press story started, a multimillion-aire real estate man left his nephew $50,000,000 provided he held a steady job until he was 35. The young man dutifully drove a bus in New Jersey for ten years. After reaching 35, he took off—literally and explosively. Today he is as happy as any man can be whose highest aspirations include an abundant supply of "bikini-clad" mates and the frivolous spending of money. His only worry: that newspaper reporters have painted him as a "sensation-minded eccentric."

What does his life story illustrate? It is a gold mine of assumptions which we tend to blow up into absolute truths. The uncle, of course, assumed that work would "make a man of him"—a "truth" that experience has not shown to be self-evident. The testator also assumed that once he had imposed his will on another person, there was a "safe" point at which pressure could be removed. But forcing another to conform to your will may produce unfortunate consequences. You may find it difficult to relax your pressure—yet you must at some point; otherwise there will not be a sufficient incentive to submit to you. A third assumption is that the chief goal in life is the accumulation of money—to be dumped like so much garbage when that goal has been attained. This, interestingly enough, is the assumption the nephew accepted in toto from his uncle. Another of the nephew's assumptions was that an artificially imposed time limit must inexorably be followed no matter what the consequences.

There are other hidden assumptions in this tale, but we will point out only one more: the reader's assumption that this story by Associated Press was true. A day after the story appeared, AP quoted the "nephew" as saying he was just "a big phony." Actually, his mother supported him. As he observed, "People are so gullible."

Moral: Your facts are built on the sands of your assumptions.

Rich Friends Can Be Costly

An old Chinese story tells about a rich man who invited his poor friend to a New Year's feast. The poor man was delighted. He knew that etiquette demanded that he bring a gift, perhaps furnish the soy sauce for the banquet. Rather than buy more, which he could not afford to do, he decided to take the flask that held his year's supply. He would take home the unused portion. How much could the guests use? The answer, unfortunately, was: every bit of it.

Moral: When you give your all to a rich man, do not assume you have a right to ask for a return.

Some people will sacrifice everything to get "a piece of the action." And the action quite often lies with men who are rich or powerful. Why people subordinate themselves to successful men and women quite often rests on hidden assumptions. Although the many types can be easily found everywhere in contemporary business and politics, to remove ourselves from the partisanship and turmoil of the present day let's go back to the 16th century and three followers of Henry VIII. The price of involvement was as costly then as it is today.

Sir Thomas More, an outstanding humanist and philosopher, assumed that serving the king was not only a way to advancement but the proper and right thing to do. Henry liked him, valued his abilities and appointed him to a number of important posts. The two men even agreed on religion—they were devout Roman Catholics, and More helped Henry write an attack on Martin Luther that won for the king the title of "Defender of the Faith" from the Pope. (It might be noted in passing that the Pope soon regretted his words and excommunicated Henry. However, the magic of labels is so great that the title has been used by every succeeding British ruler, including Queen Elizabeth II.) When Henry insisted on a divorce from his first wife, however, More was appalled. He assumed that he could resolve his dilemma by resigning as lord chancellor and retiring to the country. Henry's anger pursued him. He was imprisoned, and when he refused to take the Oath of Supremacy which declared Henry the supreme head of the Church of England, More was beheaded. More was canonized in 1935. Since saints are hard to find these days, perhaps some would say he was justly rewarded.

Now let us turn to Thomas Cromwell, Earl of Essex. Cromwell's spiritual descendants are all around us today. They are essentially second-class men, narrow in vision and obedient to their master's every wish. They are jealous of their titles and perquisites and assume that everyone (in time this includes their master) is inferior to them. Cromwell was industrious and efficient in fulfilling the king's wishes. He managed Henry's first divorce. He dissolved the monasteries (obtaining their wealth for the king, although a substantial amount stuck to his fingers). He prompted and arranged Henry's fourth marriage, to Anne of Cleves, and assumed that his blind service would be amply rewarded. Unfortunately, Anne had no looks, no accomplishments, and no dowry. The marriage was only a political arrangement, which did not last long. Cromwell had saddled the king with a plain and not overly bright wife. Naturally Henry judged this to be treason and had him beheaded.

There were, of course, other reasons for the misfortunes of More and Cromwell, but right up there on top was Anne Boleyn, a somewhat attractive woman who wouldn't give in to Henry until he got rid of his first wife and they were properly wed. He assumed she could provide him with a male heir. She assumed he was joking when he sent her to the Tower of London for treason. Both were wrong. *She* was beheaded.

Today, in an age when the Pentagon has seriously considered attaching torpedoes to dolphins and aiming them at "the enemy's" ships—relying, as Russell Baker says, on their "zeal for dying for the free world"—it may be worthwhile to compare this arrangement with a synergistic superior/subordinate relationship from a bygone day. Many

New Yorkers consider the Brooklyn Bridge to be the most beautiful structure ever built by man. Among them was John H. Dooley, an engineer with the Department of Highways for 52 years, much of that time as chief of the Division of Bridge Operations. In 1973, the bridge's ninetieth anniversary, he was given a medal by the City of New York. Although he had been retired for three years, he had continued to show up at his old job every day, working without pay to arrange for the maintenance of his beloved bridge.

Moral: You may not be able to afford the rich, but you can afford an enriched life.

Does a "Halo" Blind You?

King Leopold I of Belgium once wrote to his niece Princess Victoria that he had "Not been able to ascertain that you have really grown taller lately," but "I must recommend it strongly." Victoria apparently ignored this avuncular recommendation and never grew much over five feet tall even after she became a queen.

Our advice to children is often tainted with our own concept of importance, which is not necessarily what is important to them. Victoria recognized this and once complained to Leopold: "[I] must beg you, as you have sent me to show what a Queen *ought not* to be, that you will send me what a Queen *ought* to be."

As a rule, people tend to agree with the opinions of those they like. That is, they judge the opinion by judging the advocate of it. Conversely, even the most persuasive opinions of someone they dislike may be rejected. Many of us suffer from the "halo" effect. There are certain characteristics that we particularly admire, and when we see them in others we lose all ability to evaluate their behavior objectively or, more important, to see them as whole persons. The hero worshiper (and the person in love) suffers from the halo effect to an extreme degree. Only the positive qualities that a person wishes to see are seen. The hero's head is encircled by a halo. His feet may be in the mud, but are invisible. Decisions influenced by the halo effect are not likely to be reasonable ones. Some of the most atrocious conduct in the world is excused by saying, "I only did what 'my hero' asked me to do." Sometimes he does not even need to ask. The follower's assumption that a certain course of action will please the hero is enough. Thomas à Becket, for example, was murdered because several knights wanted to rid the king of a troublesome opponent. The king, however, was not pleased. He would have liked to see Becket humbled, but murder was more than he wanted. Quite often acts designed to please the hero are carried to extremes. The aide who frequently boasted he would "walk over my grandmother" for President Nixon impressed many not as a devoted public servant but as a fanatic. If he would do that to his poor old grandma, what might he have done to the average citizen?

A little healthy skepticism is useful in controlling the halo effect within ourselves. An example of such questioning behavior is illustrated by two competing salesmen accidentally meeting at an airport. "Where are you going?" one asked. "To New York." "Aha, I know you," the first salesman cried. "You say that you're going to New York because you want me to think that you're going to Chicago. But I happen to know that you're really going to New York. So tell me, why did you lie to me?"

Moral: Questioning yourself and others discloses assumptions.

Changeable "Human Nature"

A man who had devoted his life to God unexpectedly inherited $5 million on his fortieth birthday. He decided he would indulge a fantasy he had had for years—he wanted to look like Cary Grant. He went to Switzerland to consult a famous plastic surgeon. The doctor warned him it was possible, but that the procedure was painful and expensive and would extend over two years. The man replied: "All right. This is what I want. I can afford it."

For two years he went through a series of bone replacements and skin grafts. At the end of that time, the project was declared a success. He looked exactly like Cary Grant. He rushed out of the hospital to buy a whole new wardrobe to match his elegant new appearance. As he stepped off the curb he was hit by a car and died instantly.

When he arrived in heaven he requested an interview with God, which was granted. He entered, knelt and said, "My Lord, I have been faithful to you all my life. I was a good and devoted servant. Did you choose to take me because it was wrong of me to have such an all-consuming human desire?" God answered, "No, quite frankly I just didn't recognize you."

This is an example of the old belief that a change in appearance can change one's nature. Today many say, "You can't change human nature." Applied to a large enough group in a single society, in a given time, it is possibly a defensible statement. The group would exhibit the various acquired and inherited characteristics that have been handed down from generation to generation within their culture. When applied to an individual, the statement has little validity, yet it is often used as an excuse to maintain the status quo and to defend indefensible conduct. "Everybody does it" and "It's human nature" are variations on the same theme.

Charles A. Reich observed:

> In a technological world, which can manufacture reality at will, man cannot passively accept the so-called reality that is forced upon him . . . we are responsible for what we call reality. It is not something that is inevitable, but something we choose. And having the power to choose, we have the power to choose and to create something better. . . . The moment we acknowledge responsibility for our present condition, we regain the sacred power that human consciousness gives us, the power to choose by what truths we shall live.

In discarding a frozen view of human nature, we have to uncover the hidden assumptions that have led us to accept a limited, often negative view of life. A younger child in a large family may view his parents' love like an apple pie. If two people divide it, there is plenty for both, but as the number of the divisions grows, the portions become smaller. This is true of physical resources, but not of love. Feelings and thoughts are like the horn of plenty whose abundance is never exhausted. The more we love the more loving we become. Human beings have capacities for ideas, trust, good will and honor which when shared grow.

The transportation commissioner of Connecticut announced a major innovative change in toll-collecting methods. It would eliminate toll-evaders' speeding through without paying. In periods of heavy traffic it would permit 600 to 800 cars to pass through a lane in an hour instead of the old 300 to 350 cars. Ticket-holding commuters would no longer have to get into long lines with buses and trucks. It would create new jobs in the state, reducing unemployment. All this at a cost of $178,000 a year. The change? Replace all rented automatic toll machines with people. In 1958 when the toll machines were first put into use, the assumption was that machines could do things better, faster and more cheaply than people. It took 15 years for the state to reexamine its assumptions, but when it did, tests brought out more timely facts. At last report, the toll booths were discontinued because of the accidents to cars and toll collectors. Human attitudes can change, and often, as in this case, they can change for the better. Since human attitudes are responsible for "human nature"—that too can change. Moral: One's concept of human nature is usually the commonly accepted errors of the time.

Society of Presumed Equals

There was a wise old teacher who was asked by two pupils to adjudicate a dispute between them. After he had heard the first pupil's story, he nodded and said "You're right." The other pupil objected: "Wait a minute. Let me tell my story." So he told his version and when he was finished the wise man said, "You're right." With this, the wise man's wife, who had been listening, exploded: "How can you say that? First you say he's right. Then you say *he's* right. They can't both be right!" The wise man stroked his beard and said, "And you're right too."

Ever since Thomas Jefferson wrote the words "all men are created equal," the statement has engendered difficulties. It captured the imagination of people throughout the world, yet the existence of slavery in the United States at that time was an obvious denial of the statement. Further, no one then or now would classify Jefferson and other Founding Fathers as ordinary men. Today the dilemma seems even greater. We essentially deny the statement either by saying we must work toward the goal of equality or by claiming it is contrary to human nature. Can we ask the wise old teacher who is right?

There are many approaches to the problem of inequality in our society. At least two views can be seen, the vertical and the horizontal. Those who see the social order as a vertical organization tend to divide people into "them" and "us." "They" are down below and must be kept there. "We" are the masters of all creation whom everyone else envies. Probably every prejudice of man can be traced to this "good guys/bad guys" hierarchy. One pathetic thing about such people is that they themselves are so easily manipulated. All it takes is a demagogue to turn them into a quivering mass of fears and frustration. He needs only a few code words to produce anxiety—"law and order," "lesser breeds," "the Four Hundred"—and he can be master of a group of the "elite." An "elite" can be easily directed. Miriam Ungerer in *Good Cheap Food* gives an example in how the potato became popular in France. Late in the 18th century when all good Frenchmen turned up their noses at potatoes, Parmentier learned to love them while a prisoner of war in Prussia. When he returned to France, he persuaded Louis XVI that they were good to eat. The king planted a field of potatoes, fenced it in and posted a guard over it. Suddenly, every fashionable Frenchman wanted to eat potatoes. Today the French have more recipes for potatoes than do any other nationality. That's why, when you see "Parmentier" on an "elite" French menu you can be sure a potato is nearby.

For those who prefer to organize society in a horizontal way, equality is paramount; everyone queues up and gets his share like everyone else. But what if supplies run out? Here as in the vertical order, to be number 1 is better than being number 1,000,000. And there are other possible hitches. No matter what the system, some try to bend it. An enterprising bank depositor in Washington, D.C., figured out that the bank's computer "read" only the magnetically imprinted bank-account numbers on the deposit slips. He removed all blank deposit slips at the bank's writing desks and replaced them with his own imprinted forms. In the next three days customers using the incorrect slips, thinking they were blank, placed $100,000 in the daring depositor's account. "They" are still looking for him.

These renegades in the system are not the only obstacles to persons who want to get ahead legitimately. Possibly the greatest hurdle is the limitations that people put on themselves. In that antiquated Victorian phrase, they "know their place." And usually it is a more modest position than they are entitled to by any objective standard. It is better not to view your talents as a package deal to be ranked in a single hierarchy of values. It is only by your accord and agreement that life ranks you by its standards and hierarchies. We need faith both in ourselves and in our fellow human beings. This makes for complete social mobility: faith in ourselves to travel vertically; in others to assist us horizontally. Maybe we are all right?

Lovers of Freedom—Advocates of Power

A. M. Rosenthal, executive editor of *The New York Times*, wrote in 1986: "After so many years as a correspondent and editor, I still find myself puzzled and pained that my own country often does not act as it talks and that many of my countrymen who demand freedom for themselves don't give much of a damn about it for others."

The Reagan administration, cheered on by Attorney General Edwin Meese III, rarely saw any "legal problems" when the privacy of others was invaded. In 1985, lie detector tests were decreed for virtually every federal employee to bring an end to "security" leaks. (These are okay if they advance the administration's policy but are a "crime" when they have an adverse affect.) Most employees accepted the decree, but Secretary of State Shultz threatened to resign if anyone said "polygraph" to him. The boom in lie detector stocks then suddenly collapsed, and rumor mongering flourished again in Washington.

The following year, Rodney Smith, deputy executive director of the President's Commission on Organized Crime, became the focus of attention in Congress and what a picture it made! A very proper young man (Smith), obviously disturbed, sat before a bank of television cameras clutching an odd-shaped object.

The incident took place during a House subcommittee hearing on the commission's proposal to require urinalysis drug testing for federal, state, and local employees, as well as employees of government contractors. The subcommittee's chairman had surprised the official by holding up a small plastic jar and saying, "I think a specimen is worth 1,000 oaths," and handed him the jar and asked him to go into the men's room to produce the sample under the direct supervision of a staff member. (Military procedures for random drug tests require a witness to ensure no substitution of specimens.)

Smith denounced the request as a "cheap shot," but actually it was a dry run. Smith refused to cooperate, whereupon the chairman said, "I thank you for very eloquently proving the point that we have set out to prove."

Morals: "Sir, there have existed, in every age and every country, two distinct orders of men—the lovers of freedom and the devoted advocates of power."

—Robert V. Hayne (U.S. Senator), 1830

"Since the general civilization of mankind, I believe there are more instances of the abridgement of the freedom of the people by gradual and silent encroachments of those in power than by violent and sudden usurpations."

—James Madison, 1788

Life Situations vs. Case Studies

In the 1970's, *New York* magazine assembled a panel of pastrami lovers from among its staff and sent out for sandwiches from various eating places whose pastrami had been especially recommended. The panel then sat down to eat and evaluate. An elaborate chart with comments was made, ranking the purveyors from best to worst. A surprising number of New Yorkers have a favorite source of pastrami sandwiches, but they guard its location as though it were a state secret. So the magazine not only revealed "inside" information, it also filled up a great deal of space—perhaps more than the subject required.

A few weeks later, the food editor of *The New York Times* gleefully revealed that many of the sandwich places tested only heated the pastrami they served. It was processed and cooked by a single supplier. "The most amazing point," the supplier said, "was that you had a number of different comments—this pastrami was too salty, that was not salty enough—and it was the same item."

If the panel had viewed the situation as a slice of life rather than merely a slice of pastrami, things might have been better. The goodness of even a simple sandwich depends on more factors than the quality of the meat. How good is the bread, the mustard, the pickle? Was the meat sliced thick or thin? Was it hot or getting cold? What was the time taken for the delivery? What about the panel's appetite? That certainly didn't remain constant throughout the test.

But enough of pastrami sandwiches. How relevant is any test situation? The illustration serves to reveal some of the weaknesses inherent in the case-study method so much admired by some professors of law and business administration. In essence, these professors take a life situation, abstract the "meat" from it and discard what they regard as the nonessential "trimmings." The situation may be more readily digested by the student, but it by no means provides the sure answers which the graduate can use when later confronted with a messy, nonstructured life situation.

Work in America, a report by a Special Task Force to the Secretary of Health, Education and Welfare, discussed a typical case study in which to increase productivity, working conditions were improved for unskilled workers. The experts had no doubt that improving conditions would create a situation that would be approved by all those involved:

> The first major experiment in Norway [was] carried out in the metalworking industry, a crucial but unproductive sector of the Norwegian economy. A dilapidated wire-drawing plant was chosen for the experiment on the ground that if improvements could be realized there, they could be achieved anywhere. But production increased so much due to job redesign that the experiment was suspended: The unskilled workers in the experiment had begun to take home pay packets in excess of the most skilled workers in the firm, thus engendering bitterness.

The story in itself is dismal enough. Surely someone could have come up with a creative alternative that would have preserved the benefits of the experiment, yet satisfied the needs of the skilled workers. Yet the case-study answer doesn't lend itself to that. Unless there is a tidy solution to a tidy problem, the whole untidy life situation is often scrubbed.

People trained solely by the case-study method may not know how to take advantage of a life situation. This is the circumstance when a novice attorney steeped in law-school case-study methodology comes up against a witness who has developed a severe case of selective memory. He will feel he has done his whole duty when he conveys that he thinks the witness who says "I can't remember" is lying. The more life-seasoned lawyer may handle this type of problem differently. He realizes that life does not conform to stock assumptions and uniform answers. He knows that there are many curious bypaths that can get you farther than can the straight and narrow path of rationality.

The distinguished trial lawyer, Congressman and jurist Louis Heller relates such a happy journey in his book, *Do You Solemnly Swear?*

Q. When you say you don't remember, Mr. Jones, do you mean by that that you remembered it and forgot it, or that you never remembered it at all?

A. I remembered it and forgot it.

Q. Your accident happened on January 10, 1948, and today is March 14, 1953. I know that you cannot give me the exact date you forgot it, but you certainly can give me the year?

A. It was in 1952.

Q. Thank you for your assistance. Now that you remember that you forgot in 1952, I know that you forgot it, but can you tell me what time of year it was?

A. Some time in the middle of the year.

Q. Would it be a fair statement that it was some time between June and August? Is that what you mean by the middle of the year?

A. Yes, sir.

Q. I know you don't remember the precise time of day that you forgot it. I am sure, however, that you can tell us whether it was early morning, afternoon, or evening.

A. It was some time in the afternoon.

Q. From your answer, I take it that you forgot it in the year 1952, some time between June and August and during the afternoon? Is that right?

A. Yes, sir.

In another case, a careless assumption caused a $200,000 loss for an insurance company. In the 80's, a man who claimed he was "self-employed in marketing," applied for a life insurance policy. Since he lived in a mansion on Long Island and obviously was well-heeled, MONY was happy to oblige him.

Less than a year later he was last seen alive, heading for Boston with a half-ton cargo of marijuana in his van. Six months later his skeleton was found in a trunk.

MONY was appalled to discover that he was the head of a million-dollar pot ring and refused to pay the poor, bereft mother, saying, "A drug dealer is exposed to risks which an insurer would not want to underwrite."

In 1986, a Manhattan Supreme Court judge, asking himself "What's in a name?" consulted his dictionary and ruled, "Webster's Dictionary defines marketing," the term used in the application, as "The act of buying or selling in the market." He ordered MONY to pay up for not doing their homework.

All of this points to the fact that if you consider life an open process rather than attempting to confine it to a rigid case-study, you may arrive at more meaningful "truths." At least you will have more to work with while trying.

VI
Ideas

Ideas Have Values

People of a conservative bent are usually not overly receptive to new ideas. They tend rather to reexamine old ideas to find new values in them. They are the "old fogies" that so irritate the young and adventurous whose "new" ideas are spurned or ignored. It is a good thing to blend the caution of the conservative with the innovative thinking of the young. Not all ideas are necessarily good even though new. And many old ideas must be discarded if we are to grow. Yet they should not be discarded capriciously, without careful evaluation. When the United States was trying to decide what kind of government best suited it, ideas about monarchy and democracy were fiercely debated.

Fisher Ames, a Massachusetts statesman, was not too happy about either: "Monarchy is like a splendid ship, with all sails set; it moves majestically on, then it hits a rock and sinks forever. Democracy is like a raft. It never sinks, but, damn it, your feet are always in the water." Confronted with such a choice, Ames reluctantly opted for democracy but joined the conservative Federalist Party, where he felt his feet would be a little drier. Most people make similar compromises, for they find that life cannot be forced into a straitjacket by our failure to reexamine ideas.

Good Ideas Can Still Harm You

A British magazine for purchasing agents got a "good" idea. It wanted to increase reader response to an industry questionnaire, so it enclosed a Bulgarian 200-lev bank note as a bonus when the questionnaire was sent out. Although impressive and official-looking, the bank notes had no value outside the borders of Bulgaria. The return on the questionnaire was very good, and the idea was judged a success until one purchasing agent violently protested. He thought it was very poor business policy to send bank notes of any kind to a purchasing agent. What would members of his staff think if he should open his mail in front of them? Probably, the worst. The enclosure was discontinued.

Beware of "good" ideas. They can still harm you, sometimes irreparably. A good idea may be useful if you are out to change the world. However, if you're just interested in making money, they can delay the endeavor. Our world consists of an infinite number of variables, and to be successful and economically sound, a "good" idea must be tested out and survive all these chances. Matty Fox, a brilliant business promoter, became intrigued with what a good idea pay TV was. A person could select the type of television program he wanted and pay for it. What could be more democratic and profitable? Fox spent millions of his own dollars before he realized that a good idea does not necessarily become an economic success. Too many established forces in the entertainment field did not want competition from pay TV and were willing to battle Fox every step of the way until he gave up, broke.

It should be noted that cable TV later made Fox's idea practical and profitable. As Samuel Butler observed: "Every new idea has something of the pain and peril of childbirth about it; ideas are just as mortal and just as immortal as organized beings are.

Many of us equate a good idea with the most direct and therefore easiest way to achieve success. *The New York Times* reported that the great former pitcher Bobby Feller was being besieged by young players to show them how to throw a spitball. According to rumors, a certain pitcher was making the ball do great tricks by using the method. "Whenever I'm asked this by the kids," Feller said, "my answer is always the same. Don't bother learning. Youngsters today seem to be interested in knowing everything about pitching except how to get a fastball over the plate. That's the most important item in pitching." Feller won 266 games during his career, and the "only" thing he needed was that concept and lots of skill and practice. It isn't a fancy idea or good idea, but it's one that produces results over and over again.

Moral: If you want profits, seek the workable.

Timely Ideas

In his bitter years of exile, Napoleon observed that if he had been hit by a cannonball while riding into Moscow, he would have gone down as the greatest man in history. Some might award this honor to Alexander the Great, who did have the good sense to die at an early age, having never lost a battle in Europe, Africa, or Asia.

Like conquering heroes, ideas also have their ups and downs. Victor Hugo once wrote, "Greater than the tread of mighty armies is an idea whose time has come." Whenever the U.S. Congress after years of procrastination and delay finally is compelled to adopt an innovative idea, the great surrender is signaled by the former opposition's intoning, "This is an idea whose time has come." Which means it could no longer be stopped.

When it comes to new ideas, many people firmly believe that any change will adversely affect their insulated lives. They may well be right. Yet no one can realistically expect to isolate himself from the world and from changing ideas. A typical example was the New York State legislator who decided the short-lived fad of "streaking" offered such an opportunity. Therefore he asked the State Senate to express its "disapproval, dismay and abhorence" of the "uncivilized practice of 'streaking.' " Presumably he felt that with senators like him, Rome would never have declined, let alone fallen. Most assuredly he felt the voters in his district would be impressed by his stand.

Novel ideas can occasionally become established ones. At the end of World War II, when people had plenty of money and very little to spend it on, ballpoint pens made their phenomenally successful debut. Later improvements have blurred the memory of how bad the original pens really were. Yet their novelty was only one aspect of the success. The "market" was already there, a market waiting to be exploited. That time it worked. More often it doesn't. Fashions in clothing, for example, seek to exploit trends and tastes. Many a clothing manufacturer's road to ruin in the 1960's was strewn with Nehru jackets and that "answer" to the miniskirt, the maxi.

A timely idea usually rests on a broader base than novelty. The original concept is sound, and the public need for the idea has begun to emerge and can be reinforced. Take Daniel F. Gerber as an example. His father and he ran a small canning company in Michigan. When the younger Gerber's daughter became ill, the doctor suggested strained peas in her diet. At the time, strained baby food was sold in pharmacies on doctor's prescriptions. Gerber quickly found out that putting peas through a strainer by hand was a drag. So he introduced canned strained baby food to groceries at 15 cents rather than the 35-cent prescription price. He was careful to get approval of doctors for his products. When he brought some of his first products to a Detroit pediatrician, the doctor said, "You don't realize what you have there. I never knew Henry Ford and I always wanted to meet a multimillionaire." The doctor's prognosis was correct.

Most people do not have the patience or persistence to carefully evaluate their needs and the needs of a market. They seize upon a novel idea and try to exploit it. One such misguided individual walked into a Bronx bank, pointed a gun at a woman teller, demanded money, and warned her not to duck and trigger the alarm. The teller ducked and set off the alarm, and the robber fled.

Moral: If you insist on trying to victimize someone, beware of the alternatives your victim may come up with—especially if you suggest them.

As a postscript to the above, a few days later the same man returned to the same bank but was thoughtful enough to go to a different window. Unfortunately, the same teller was there, so he told her, "If you push the alarm I'll kill you." She ducked and pushed the alarm. He fled.

Moral: If a "good" idea doesn't work, don't retreat to the familiar. Try a different idea or a different career.

Experiments in Ideas

Although some of us realize the limitation of status quo ideas, we quite often see certain past eras as Golden Ages. If we look only at isolated segments of the past, in fact, this may well seem true. One such segment is the world of ideas in Colonial America before the Revolution. And a great "idea man" of the period was Benjamin Franklin. His ideas are still appreciated and interesting today because they were conceived at a time when the world was on the threshold of the modern scientific era. Every observation, every fact could stimulate new ideas about why things happen. Today most of us feel, in the area of ideas, somewhat like the last shopper Saturday night at the supermarket. Everything that's left has been picked over and discarded by countless people before us. It might be worth a look at what Franklin found interesting and how he assembled his observations into ideas that still have merit today.

On Experiments in Electricity: "The person so struck sinks down doubled or folded together as it were, the joints losing their strength and stiffness at once, so that he drops in the spot where he stood, instantly, and there is no previous staggering, nor does he ever fall lengthwise. Too great a charge might, indeed, kill a man, but I have not yet seen any death done by it. It would certainly, as you observed, be the easiest of all deaths."

On the Origin of Northeast Storms (the Southwest): "We were to have an eclipse in Philadelphia, on a Friday evening about 9 o'clock. I intended to observe it, but was prevented by a northeast storm, which came on about 7, with thick clouds as usual, that quite obscured the whole hemisphere. When the post brought us the Boston newspaper giving the accounts of the effects of the same storm in these parts, I found that the beginning of the eclipse had been well observed there [before the storm began], though Boston lies northeast of Philadelphia about 400 miles.

"Thus to produce northeast storms, I suppose some great heat or rarefaction of the air in or about the Gulf of Mexico; the air thence rising has its place supplied by the next more northern, cooler, and therefore denser and heavier, air, etc., in a successive current, to which our coast and inland ridge of mountains give the direction of northeast, as they lie northeast and southwest."

On Daylight Saving Time: Franklin and a group of friends in Paris were taken with a new oil lamp that gave much more light than ordinary lamps. But there was a question as to how much oil it would consume. If it consumed that much more oil in giving that much more light, then there was no economy. "I was pleased to see this general concern with the economy . . . for I love economy exceedingly." He records that he went home thinking about this constantly. At about six o'clock in the morning suddenly a noise woke him up, at which time he was amazed that his room was ablaze with sunlight. It was amusing that Franklin, who affected a great simplicity in clothing and manner, should have been surprised at this. Apparently Paris attractions had made him forget his own words "Early to bed and early to rise, makes a man healthy, wealthy, and wise" (*Poor Richard's Almanack*, 1733—many years before). Then he decided that what had been happening with him as well as most Parisians was that they spent six hours in bed in the morning when the sun was up and at night they used six hours' worth of candlepower. He wrote this to the *Journal of Paris* and made a calculation of how much would be saved by the 100,000 families of Paris if they got up earlier in the summer and utilized the first six hours of the sun instead of lighting six hours of the evening. And he made his calculation: "An immense sum, that the city of Paris may save every year by the economy of using sunlight instead of candles."

Although very few of us can expect to make very significant similar scientific observations, we still have a chance, for example, to observe ourselves and others in human behavior modes. Such will facilitate our ability to form new ideas in this and other areas.

As an example, a group of New Jersey legislators thought they had hit on a constructive new idea when they proposed to make inmates at the state prison eligible for parole after six months. To their astonishment, the Rahway Prisoners Council told them the legislation was "frivolous." The members of the council felt that every inmate should serve at least one year, but that during that time he should be given psychological guidance and the opportunity to improve his education or learn a job skill. They felt that anyone serving only a six-month term should not be in state prison at all. "He should be kept in a community-based facility near home so his family isn't destroyed. . . ." This is the kind of innovative rethinking of an age-old problem that Benjamin Frankin would be proud of.

Differences and Meanings of Ideas

Mark Van Doren once defined a tragedy as a quarrel in which both sides are right. We are so used to seeing issues as opposites that we refuse to entertain the thought that both sides can be right and yet disagree. One such impasse occurred at a New York publishing house when management decided that female fashion had got out of hand. It issued a memo:

> Bare feet, bare midriffs, bare backs, halter necklines, spaghetti straps, micro-mini skirts, shorts and culottes, tank tops, T-shirts, undershirts, AND SUCH, which are in the fashion picture, may be acceptable modes of dress (or lack of it) for picnics, poolside, beach and cookouts, but they are totally UNacceptable in an office environment.

Following the New Testament injunction "Let not the sun go down upon your wrath," the staff immediately fired off this reply memo:

> Pillbox hats, veils, white gloves, stockings with seams, closed front and back shoes, matching shoes and handbags, skirts at the middle of the knee, Pan-cake make-up, bras, girdles, Merry Widows, trusses, vaginal sprays, Evening in Paris perfume—while they were perfectly acceptable modes of attire in 1940 and for elderly spinsters, they are totally UNacceptable for employees of the publisher of *The Happy Hooker*, *Deep Throat* and *Last Tango*.

In this interplay we can see that wrong ideas can be traditional ideas gone stale. They no longer meet current needs.

We are, for example, so accustomed to paying by check rather than cash, it should surprise no one that some have forgotten the difference. An actress in New York City was forced to write a check to two teen-age girl muggers when they found she had only $4 in cash. Everything ran along traditional lines: they asked for $40 but settled for $25. Instead of the check being made out to Cash, one of the teen-agers insisted it be made out to her personally. It was later discovered that she patronized a check-cashing establishment right in the neighborhood. There her address was on file, ready for the police when they arrived.

Peter Drucker in *Management: Tasks, Responsibilities, Practices* deplores the emphasis in the management sciences on "minimizing risk" or even "eliminating risk." "The attempt to eliminate risks, even the attempt to minimize them, can only make them irrational and unbearable. It can only result in the greatest risk of all: rigidity.

Rigidity is a mental condition most of us suffer from to a considerable extent. We rely on the customary and traditional in our lives to save us from the inconvenience of constantly reexamining our ideas, thus reassuring ourselves that we have "right" ideas.

What could be "righter" than *Seventeen* magazine's decision to commission "a two-part novelet" based on a popular television series? The writer, of course, would be the one who had done the TV treatment. It sounds sensible until you realize that the TV series was based on *Tom Brown's School Days*, published in 1857, by Thomas Hughes. What makes the idea "wrong" is that *Seventeen* followed traditional thinking by moving forward to a new interpretation of a successful idea. But it failed to move back to a reexamination of the basic ideas that ensured the success of a second-generation idea. Who knows? Perhaps if they had read the original, they might have found it was just what they wanted—and saved a writer's fee: the copyright had long since run out.

It is possible to stagger through life with ideas continually proving wrong, but people who do not even bother to look for ideas have great difficulty in coping with life's daily problems. An example occurred when a snowstorm—by no means a record one—hit New York City. To no one's surprise, the Long Island Rail Road gave up as the first snowflake fell. A spokesman said, "There may be some trains moving somewhere in the system, but I just don't know where right now." The passengers spoke of their harrowing experiences: sitting in stalled trains for 12 hours or more with temperatures near freezing, toilets overflowing and railroad employees ignoring their questions. According to all accounts, the passengers were very brave. They didn't panic. They couldn't have acted more properly if they had been on the *Titanic*.

One lady, however, did not conform to the usual pattern. She found herself in a car that had been stalled for almost four hours, watching "executives who were all playing pitch-penny and none of them asking what the problem was. I wondered how much they really wanted to get where they were going." Finally she got one man to open the door and let down the steps. She walked down the slope, followed by the executives, and found herself a block from a subway stop and a few minutes from work. This woman with ideas of her own was the only one in the whole car who did not act like a sheep on the way to the slaughterhouse. Francis Bacon realized this principle in writing, "He that will not apply new remedies must expect new evils."

Successful people are not the ones who retreat to the comforting games and attitudes of childhood when confronted with a problem. They have ideas freshly burnished and ready to confront new or difficult situations. They try to know what they are doing and why. Some even achieve the lucidity of Samuel Goldwyn when he commented on accusations that he was a publicity hound:

> People say that whenever I have a picture coming out I always start a controversy about something that gets into the papers. Well, in all sincerity, I want to assure you that, as a general proposition, there's not a single word of untruth in that.

Moral: Differences can arise because of our way of thinking: our conclusions are based on our premises, our premises are based on our conclusions. We think we mean what we think.

VII
Knowing

The Observer Affects the Observed

Some years ago a Long Island boy who was studying weather and air currents received some very exciting news. One of the helium-filled balloons he had launched three days before had found its way across the Atlantic and touched down in a London garden. This information was contained in a note from the finder, who had used the self-addressed envelope attached to the balloon. When the boy announced what had happened and showed the letter, the story made the front page of *The New York Times*. Only a few days later, a small item buried in the back of *The New York Times* admitted the story had been a hoax. An airline pilot who also lived on Long Island had found the balloon 15 miles from the boys' home, had taken the envelope to London with him on his next flight, and had mailed the note from there. The postmark on the letter had convinced everyone.

All too often in life our ideas and thoughts are formed by what we permit our senses to observe selectively. This selective viewing is dictated in part by our prejudices and past and is a reason for adamant "differences of opinion" about almost any subject. One man's "crook and horse thief" is another's "distinguished senator" and a third person probably has never heard of the man. Or take the popular but anonymous rhyme of 1893:

> Lizzie Borden took an ax
> And gave her mother forty whacks;
> When she saw what she had done
> She gave her father forty-one!

This verse appeared shortly after Miss Borden was acquitted, so obviously many people disagreed with the jury. They still do, almost a hundred years later, only now the emphasis has changed from ignoring certain facts to trying to explain them away. One of the hardest to get around is that in spite of "81 whacks," Lizzie had not a drop of blood on her clothes. One writer offered the startling idea that the straitlaced Miss Borden had committed the murder in the nude. A fact that has been reported, yet never given the attention it might deserve, is that cold mutton broth was on the Borden breakfast menu that fateful day. Surely for some this alone could have provided sufficient motive for murder.

Would an actor act if there were no one to see or hear him? Probably. After all, he can act for his most appreciative audience—himself. But most actors, amateur or professional, prefer as wide an audience as they can get, and they can get it on television. In the early days of TV, many stores had closed-circuit units set up in their display windows so that window-shoppers could see themselves on television. It was extraordinary the variety of roles people played—from feigned indifference to exuberant exhibitionism. Yet each person was playing a role, his behavior affected by the fact that he was on camera. As TV self-viewers became more sophisticated (or cynical), "spontaneous" performances were directed as carefully as a Broadway hit. Thus at the 1968 Democratic National Convention in Chicago, demonstrations were the "in" thing. An ABC producer explained how it worked: "You get together and ask them [demonstration leaders], 'What are you going to do today?' and they say, 'What do you want us to do?' You say, 'I can't tell you anything,' but pretty soon you've got things worked out in a code that works for everybody." (Quoted in *New York* magazine.)

But the broad TV audience that shapes so much of what is observed should not blind us to the fact that the observed has always been shaped by the observer. It is a circular process. One of the most important aspects of dealing with people is to recognize that all have been individual in their selecting and ordering of facts that they observe. Therefore their overall perception of a particular situation will always be truly unique. This view today is opening advanced physicists to Eastern philosophy.

Four baseball umpires were having an animated discussion about their profession. When they began to talk about strikes and balls, the first said, "I calls them as they are." The second, "I calls them as I sees them." The third, "They ain't nothing till I calls them." The last said, "When I calls them, what a game!"

These four diverse approaches have made four different games out of one.

Moral: The results of your observations filter what you the viewer will see.

The Way a Cookie Crumbles

A lady in Detroit took a batch of homemade cookies to the post office and tried to mail them to a friend at the Michigan Court of Appeals in Lansing. She winced when the postal clerk slammed the package with a hand stamp. The clerk noticed her agonized expression and "knew" at once that the package contained a bomb. He confiscated the package and called the bomb squad. She was arrested, the package was opened, and the crushed cookies were discovered. Now the cops knew the truth. She was released. What no one knew, however, was that the batch of cookies and the experience were worth $1,000— the settlement the lady and the city agreed to for her false-imprisonment suit. The clerk presumably continues to crush cookies and other fragile items as he knows best how to do.

Although a number of people have won success by "sticking to their last," most of us are aware that a single nugget of knowledge is not sufficient to bring us to a satisfactory conclusion. Thus we are not surprised when "boy wonders" rise on Wall Street when the market climbs for a long period of time—and fall with a sickening thud when stocks decline. Yet everyone is inclined to look for and find the "easy" single solution. Once morphine, an opium derivative, was thought to be the "perfect" answer to the use of opium. It was a better pain reliever and was thought to be nonaddictive. When this was found not to be the case, a new drug, heroin, derived from morphine, was thought to be the answer. According to one story, it got its name from French cancer patients who called it *"héroïne"* because it could deaden the most intense pain. But it proved to be not only four to eight times more powerful than morphine but also more habit-forming. In more recent years methadone has been administered to reduce the craving of heroin addicts. Some indication of methadone's success might perhaps be that New York and New Jersey medical authorities thereafter announced that in their areas methadone passed heroin as a definite cause of narcotics deaths.

Moral: Life rarely asks questions we have the answers to.

How Do You Know Me Like You Do?

The Cajuns of Louisiana, along with the mountain people of the Ozarks and some New Englanders, are notoriously reluctant to talk to strangers until they have sized them up.

Roy Reed tells the story of the stranger who asks a Cajun how to find a man named No No LeBlanc:

> "No No LeBlanc, lessee, yeah, you go fo' about a mile dare an' you gonna see dat li'l yellow house where he live."
>
> The stranger thanks him and the Cajun says, "Wait, No No LeBlanc, you say?"
>
> "Yes."
>
> "Dat don't right, No No live on de island part of him. You got to brought you' se'f roun' de behin' side an' you gonna see a li'l yellow house wit' chinaball tree. Dass where he live."
>
> "Thank you very much."
>
> "Wait a minute. You specify No No LeBlanc, hanh?"
>
> "That's right."
>
> "Well, dass me. Whut you want?"

Many times our attempts to gain knowledge face similar frustrating delays. We have a general idea of where we want to go: we want to find out about a situation that requires fresh thinking, and we have to amass new data so that we can arrive at an intelligent decision. Yet for much of the information we must rely on our ability to communicate with all kinds of people and understand not only what they say but why they say it.

One of the saddest items in the news in the '70s was this Reuters dispatch from Geneva: "The 25-nation Geneva disarmament conference, which opened its summer session last week after a seven-week recess, met for only four minutes today—because no one wanted to speak." Some may say, if experienced diplomats can find nothing to say about banning chemical warfare and underground nuclear tests, can anyone gain anything from mere talk? Yes, we can gain insight and knowledge. Talk is capable of lifting our minds out of the ruts of complacency that they have settled into and enabling us, with our newfound stimulation, to approach our problems with a fresh outlook.

Through talk we offer points of view. Faubion Bowers notes:

> In Cambodia women cut their hair short. In Burma they smoke cigars. In China men wear gowns and women long pants. India, a country without "chefs," has the men cook and the women lay bricks. Balinese men squat to urinate and women stand. Japanese men shave with hot water in winter and ice water in summer. In the tropics you drink hot tea and eat blistering chilies to keep cool, homeopathically. Japanese fry ice cream; and while they eat fish raw they cook their oysters . . . and seaweed. In Indonesia it's the custom for men to dance in public with men to show they are not homosexual. Filipinos relish purple potatoes made into ice for dessert. In general, apart from the Westernized class, Asians begin a meal with a sweet to cut the edge of hunger, and at the end, to wash it all down, have soup. And ever since the British introduced the violin to India, a hundred years ago, musicians have played it sitting down and holding it between the shoulder and the sole of the foot. Why? Or why not?

It would be interesting to see a translation of this passage into an Asian language. How could one convey its true meaning except by presenting a mirror image—starting, "In the United States . . ."? Otherwise it would seem only commonplace to an Oriental. Thus it is with most points of view. They may serve the person who holds them, but they are like slides prepared for a microscope: they illuminate one small portion of a very complex life process.

When people disagree but don't want to argue about it, they may say, "It depends on your point of view." And indeed it does. When a Women's Lib Movement figure says, "That's the way a male-chauvinist pig looks at it," she is defining not a man's point of view but her own.

This is not to say that points of view are not important in our search for knowledge. They are. They reveal the assumptions, hidden and otherwise, on which another person relies and acts. This can be very valuable information if we use it in our consideration of how to deal with others. But it can be a positive curse if we use it to make absolute labels: "All women are alike," "All politicians are crooked," "Everyone's just out to get all he can." The resulting witches' brew adds nothing to our knowledge; it merely limits our choice in handling life situations.

It is a well-known fact that Columbus discovered America in 1492—well, it was actually a small island in the Caribbean, but that's good enough—and later discovered numerous other islands and cruised off the coast of South America. But only Europeans would call Columbus a discoverer. The Indians knew America was there all along. In the end the European point of view prevailed, and with it that old European assumption, "Finders, keepers." The Indians were left to figure out the rest of that old rhyme.

Many complain that they are victims of their points of view, but as such they do not deserve much sympathy. They are like the lady in Henry Fielding's novel *Jonathan Wild:* "[He] ravished this fair creature, or at least would have ravished her, if she had not, by a timely compliance, prevented him." Through open-mindedness we can control our points of view. They should not control us.

Moral: A point of view shapes knowing.

Lobotomized Knowing

In the mid-1960's, an eminent Soviet chemist announced the discovery of "polywater," a substance that was so dense that one could poke a hole in it, and that flowed so slowly it resembled oil in viscosity. There was much consternation in some Western countries about what the "polywater gap" might mean in the Cold War. Finally the panic subsided when Western scientists began to pooh-pooh the idea, suggesting that the water was not new but merely contaminated. The Soviet scientist vigorously defended his discovery, but finally after seven years of research agreed that the other scientists were right and he was wrong.

On both sides, outmoded patterns of thought were able to overcome years of training in the scientific method: the initial Western reaction was triggered at the time by the fear of Russian superiority in space research, the "missile gap" and other bogeymen that politicians, scientists, and the Pentagon have used and continue to use to achieve sometimes dubious goals. The Soviet scientist seems to have suffered in a most uncommunistic way from pride of ownership.

Before the discovery of tranquilizers and psychic energizers, prefrontal lobotomy was the "in thing" in surgery. The nerves of the frontal lobes of the brain were severed to relieve various mental disorders. It may have helped control some cases, but the surgery was irreversible. Most of us do not have to undergo delicate surgery to achieve the effects of lobotomization. We deliberately cut ourselves off from areas of our brain that we decide (or let others decide for us) are "irrelevant." There is no attempt to think about thinking and about knowing what is relevant. The result can be as unrewarding as the college team that sport recruiters put together. Although the team won a national championship, its epitaph was "They could do everything with a basketball but autograph it." This was a case pure and simple of the exploitation of poor and ignorant young men by adults whose zeal for making money for the college (and themselves) somehow was sealed off from what most of us regard as the college's primary function: to provide higher education. But often this goal also is perverted by students who mark time to get a degree, not because they thirst for knowledge but because a lot of employers wouldn't hire a washroom attendant without a degree. Jessica Mitford in *Kind and Usual Punishment* quotes a California state employee as estimating that it costs as much to keep a man in San Quentin as it would cost to send him to Harvard. However, unless a student is mature enough to know why he wants an education, he might not be able to distinguish between the two institutions.

Others cut themselves off from common sense and "reality" by an arrogant intolerance of new ideas. If games are not played by their rules, they are not to be played at all. The adult managers of the New Jersey Little Leagues produced a classic example in 1974. Because the New Jersey Civil Rights Division ruled that girls could not legally be excluded from the Little Leagues, the officials, in a pet, scratched the season. As one said: "We don't want girls playing this game with boys." Fortunately, it takes a long time for children to be trained to "think narrow." Little League or no Little League, girls today play ball if they want to, and if a girl is good she will pick the boys to play with.

Knowing When to Stop

Many years ago an old Jewish man was on his deathbed. His friends and relatives were gathered around him. Suddenly he opened his eyes, looked up at the sad faces and said, "I would like to eat a wormy plum." The onlookers were horrified. A wormy plum was unkosher (unclean). So they asked him why after living such a religious life he chose this moment to commit a sin. "I'm sorry," he replied, "my life has not been as holy as it may appear. As a matter of fact, I've committed many, many sins. And now I am anxiously preparing to go before my Maker. The Book of Life will be before Him. The archangel will read off all of my sins. When he comes to the part where I have eaten a plum with a worm in it, at least I'll know that he's finished."

Many people might enhance their probability of success if they could plant a "stop" order in their mind to tell them the end has come. Allan Lakein in *How to Get Control of Your Time and Your Life* says:

> . . . when executives find themselves on a treadmill they tend to lose perspective on what's important. They spend time unnecessarily on secondary matters and let many important ones go undone. . . . The more overtime they put in, the more exhausted—and the less efficient—they

become. The answer is not to spend more hours on the project but to work more effectively within the time allotted.

Use of time is very important to success. Allocation of time is essential and so is knowing the cutoff time. Whenever one is involved in a project, one should always be open to the thought of when it is time to stop. If you give up too soon, all the work that you have done is lost and there may still be success in the future. Success can be how long it takes to succeed. However, if you continue on the project indefinitely, you are wasting very valuable time that could be better spent elsewhere. There are those who work on a problem until it becomes a monomania that dominates their lives to the exclusion of everything else. Only occasionally does this kind of persistence pay off. A compulsive gambler can tell you that. Often the substitution of luck for creative thought distorts life and makes the living of it far less dependable.

Samuel Clemens' involvement in the James W. Paige typesetting machine (a "mechanical marvel," he said, which made "all the other wonderful inventions of the human mind . . . sink pretty nearly into commonplace") is a case in point. Even in its early development, the machine was doing the work of four men, and in time its output almost trebled. Justin Kaplan in *Mr. Clemens and Mark Twain* points out the fatal flaw: "until he saw it in action [in 1880] Clemens had not believed such a machine could exist. . . . Actually, the Planotype, a similar machine designed by Henry Bessemer, the inventor of the process that converts pig iron into steel, was used to set type commercially as early as 1842; a number of other machines since then had seen limited practical service . . . all of them, including the one Mark Twain backed, represented successively intricate elaborations, unworkably delicate and temperamental, of the same outmoded principle. These machines were designed to imitate the work of a man setting, justifying, and distributing single foundry types by hand. Actually, type distribution . . . was no longer necessary or practical. . . ." At the end of a press run, printers using the rotary typecaster simply melted the type down instead of distributing it (returning each sort to its proper place in the case). "This bypass of the human analogy was the basic principle of Ottmar Mergenthaler's Linotype machine.

. . . A mechanical typesetter would have to *think* in order to work, Clemens persisted in believing, and the machine he saw . . . appeared to be able to think." Paige continued to search for the "perfect" machine, and Clemens continued to back him—to the tune of about $3,000 a week—before the machine was finally abandoned and Clemens was financially ruined. In 14 years of dealing with the machine and its equally erratic inventor, Clemens could not and would not stop.

Moral: In the end there was knowing.

VIII
Creativity

Creativity Can Be Sparked

A college professor was offered a wonderful opportunity—one that could not be turned down. She was awarded a grant by a foundation to do scholarly work abroad. The only problem was, it was during the middle of the school year. How could she finish up the classes she had started? It occurred to her to make tape recordings of her remaining lectures and give them as assignments to the class. It was worth the try. The professor told her classes that she was leaving and that during the subsequent month her lextures would be on tape, which would be played at regular class hours, and they could take notes from these.

Her first canned class commenced two days before she was scheduled to leave. She could not resist the temptation to see how it was going along. She tiptoed to the classroom door and opened it. There was the tape recorder running in the front of the classroom. And in the students' seats were fifteen tape recorders diligently operating. The professor had felt creative in coming up with her solution. She was, but so were her students in responding to a new situation.

Moral: Creativity inspires creativity.

Retreating to the Familiar

A U.S. District Court judge once imposed an unusual punishment. He sentenced four men to lifelong poverty instead of prison terms. The four, who had defrauded noncommissioned officers' clubs in Vietnam, were ordered to perform charitable work and to turn over all present and future assets to the government. They were allowed to keep only their government pensions and whatever they were able to earn from daily labor. Although terming it "probably illegal," the men accepted the sentence. Some people do not need the prompting of a judge to sentence themselves to poverty. They do it every time they are confronted by a crisis. Their response is to retreat to the familiar. Instead of making an improvised or differentiated response, they find solace in performing routine duties that require little energy and even less thought. Life itself seems to stand still while they convalesce. Since a great amount of our available time is already devoted, of necessity, to the routine, this results in a disporportionate decrease in creativity. For those who are convinced only by mathematical proof, suppose we assign arbitrary but warranted differential hourly values of $5 for creative work, $2 for neutral and $1 for routine. Suppose further we examine 100 hours of work and we ascertain that we spend 15 percent of our time on creative work, 20 percent on neutral and 65 percent on routine. Suppose then that you retreat to the familiar, and routine work goes up 8 percent at the expense of the creative work, which goes down from 15 to 7 percent. The value of the creative work has declined from $75 to $35, while the value of routine work has risen by only $8, causing a loss of $32. If, on the other hand, you were to increase creative work at the expense of routine work by 15 percent, the value of creative work would increase 100 percent to $150, while the value of routine work would decrease by only $15.

Stockholders use the term "leverage" when they talk about buying stocks on margin. They tend to minimize the fact that leverage can operate for or against you depending on whether the market rises or falls. As we have seen, an increase in creativity does not have this double-edged effect. The leverage is there, but in this case it almost always operates to your advantage.

Moral: Creativity multiplies.

The Little Things in Life

Most of us have a hard enough time evolving a mental conceptualization of the world that will encompass all the "facts" as we know them. It is a rare person who can accommodate more than one such concept, and rarer still is one whose fresh vision of the world revolutionizes man's patterns of thought. Aristotle, Galileo, Freud, and Einstein were of this select breed. There are only a relatively few others. For most of us, creativity usually consists in developing and improving a little thing. This still may be enough to change life patterns in much of the world, but it is based on recognizing and exploiting a very small element of the living process. Creativity can rest on putting a little thing into a new relationship or order with other little things. It is how we relate to them, how we order them, how we structure them that helps our lives take on a new significance. Too many of us try to make our lives more creative by waiting for the "big chance." We fail to realize that the chance is, more often than not, composed of a series of little things that we let pass by from moment to moment.

Nothing is more common and unremarkable in this world than carbon. It is an essential element, however, found in all living things. After testing literally hundreds of materials, Thomas A. Edison found that carbon was the best substance to use in electric-light filaments. Although we think of carbon as an easily burnable fuel, it has a high melting point. It was this little detail that enabled Edison to perfect the first practical electric light. Although carbon has long since been replaced by tungsten wire, this should be considered an improvement rather than a creative act. Tungsten has a high melting point (higher than that of carbon) and is not prohibitively expensive—two of the criteria that had led Edison to his use of carbon in the first place.

Moral: Creativity is not limited by large or small.

Being on the Outside Can Pay

Although it's difficult to believe, until he revealingly testified before the Ervin Committee in the Watergate scandal, John Dean III was held in such high regard at the White House that testimony at another Senate hearing, stating that Dean had "probably lied" to the FBI, brought this indignant emotional response from a White House spokesman:

> The statement that Mr. Dean called Mr. Gray is absolutely correct. And I suppose I would do the same thing if it was suggested—that—well, I suppose any individual would make a phone call such as that if it had been indicated that the individual, as the exchange stated, probably lied for the purpose of making sure that those who were involved in that discussion, a discussion which resulted, of course, in extensive reports of that—and I am not being critical of that—said that Mr. Dean probably lied.

Syntax is not the only thing that suffers when we permit our emotions to take over. Coherence and creative answers also fall by the wayside. To restore the balance, it is helpful to get as far outside the problem as is possible, separating our extreme emotions from it as we increase our distance. This can be done by breaking the problem down into its discrete parts; it is difficult to become emotionally involved in one simple "fact." An old shaggy-dog story illustrates how this is done.

A young man since early childhood had suffered from an unreasoning terror of blini, the Russian pancakes filled with caviar and sour cream. An aunt decided to cure him by leading him through all the steps of preparing blini.

"First I scald the milk and let it cool. Does that frighten you?"

"No."

"Now I add the yeast. Does that frighten you?"

"No."

"Next I stir in egg yolks, salt, sugar and melted butter. Does that frighten you?"

"No."

"Now I beat the egg whites and fold them in. Does that frighten you?"

"No."

"Now I bake the batter on the griddle. Does that frighten you?"

"No."

"Finally I add caviar and sour cream and roll them up—"

"Blini!!!" the young man screamed as he passed out.

If we find it difficult to get outside of a problem, then it may be time to call for assistance—preferably from someone who has not been involved in the particular problem but has encountered many like it. By definition he should be emotionally uninvolved. That is why a doctor must be psychoanalyzed before he is permitted to practice psychiatry. Otherwise he would project his own neuroses on his future patients.

When we look for advice, we should seek a person who is concerned with our problem but not involved; interested but not prejudiced; one who can relate to but not be inundated by the situation.

One of the myths of our age is that the "insider" has a built-in advantage over the "outsider." This is sometimes true, especially where the market price of a company's stock is involved. Once a young man completely involved physically and emotionally in the development of a new product for a large corporation advised a close friend to buy the company's stock immediately. The friend, instinctively distrusting the emotional involvement, hesitated. The stock went from 30 to 60 in a short time, and the friend never stopped berating himself for not taking advantage of the opportunity. Two ironical facts were involved in the situation: first, the new product failed to meet its promise; and second, over the years, as the friend lamented his failure to double his money, the stock's value further increased nonetheless to 150 and better. Not only do some people tend to lose control of emotions; they often get emotional about other people's emotions. In both cases they forfeit much.

Another modern myth is that in this age of conglomerates, the individual counts for nothing. John Kenneth Galbraith generalizes when he says: "There is no more pleasant fiction than that technical change is the product of the matchless ingenuity of the small man forced by competition to employ his wits to better his neighbors. Unhappily, it is a fiction. Technical development has long since become the preserve of the scientist and the engineer. Most of the cheap and simple inventions have, to put it bluntly, been made."

Like most generalizations, this is too general. Progress or failure in any field is made by individuals, not corporations. An obituary of Laurens Hammond in 1973 cited among his achievements the invention of the electric organ, the electric clock, and "a barometer that could be sold for $1." Other inventions that were developed outside the "organization" include the jet engine, Kodachrome, air conditioning, FM radio, and the Xerox copier. Then too, individuals run conglomerates, just as conglomerates run people. We hear very little of those who work for the multinational corporations—but when we do! In July 1973, *The New York Times* reported:

> Last month, when a multinational Swiss corporation announced plans to abolish the jobs of nearly half of the work force at a watch factory it owns in France—the Lip Company in Besançon—the workers seized the plant and continue to turn out watches, selling them at cut-rate prices. . . . The Roman Catholic Archbishop of Besançon told the largest demonstration the town has seen since the Liberation in 1945, "I know what the imperatives are of a modern economy. But have we not resigned ourselves too quickly to make of money the master of the world?"

Making Your Dreams Work

The late Dr. Kilton Stewart, a psychotherapist, made a detailed and trail-blazing study of dream education. He worked with the Senoi, a small tribe of hunters and fishers in the Malay peninsula jungles. They had allegedly adopted a form of dream education and developed a sophisticated dream culture beyond Western achievements. He discovered that although the dreams of the Senoi children revealed the same aberrating patterns as those of contemporary Western man, this was not true in the adults. He noted: "At the same time, [the dream education] reorganizes and restructures the personality. This form of psychology enables the dream process to keep the foundations of the wakeful mind in contact with, and under the control of, the self-regulating center as it operates in sleep."

Later, Stewart observed, "In the West the thinking we do while asleep usually remains on a muddled, childish, or psychotic level because we do not respond to dreams as socially important and include dreaming in the educative process."

How dream education can help us cope with life is far too complex to explore adequately here. We can, however, examine one of its aspects: problem solving. This can be used profitably by many who now think that the human mind stops thinking of problems when we sleep. The method has been used by a number of people with varying degrees of success: While lying in bed before going to sleep, think about your problem. Do not get involved with alternative and possible solutions. Just present the problem to yourself in as clear and concise a form as possible. Then forget about it and go to sleep. Some people like to have a pencil and pad beside their bed so that if they wake up in the middle of the night with an alternative solution, they can immediately jot it down. Such a solution in many instances is adequate. It is, however, less likely to be as complete and satisfactory as a solution arrived at in the morning and after a full night's sleep.

William James in his studies in psychology and religion tells of an experience he had while in a trancelike state induced by inhaling ether: Suddenly he was seized with a thought that seemed to hold the ultimate truth about the universe, roused himself and quickly wrote it down. Later, when he was fully conscious, he read what he had written: "The smell of ether pervades everything." The thought, of course, encompassed the "universe" of James's experience at the moment, but the "truth" hardly had a practical application. Our morning solutions can often be more valuable than those middle-of-the-night ones or solutions evolved through constant thinking and worrying while awake. Postnight solutions bring into play hidden resources with problem-solving potentialities that most of us do not know even exist.

Senoi children are encouraged to pursue a dream to its completion so that they can come to terms with its content, whether it be frightening (a "falling" dream) or pleasant (an erotic dream).

When a child reports to his Senoi parents a falling dream, they will congratulate him, say it was a fine dream and ask did he bring back any discoveries from the place he fell to? If he said he was frightened and awoke before landing, the parents would explain that all dreams have a purpose. The spirit might want to grant him some powers, so that he should relax and enjoy such dreams and bring back a discovery such as a song or dance.

Stewart sets a goal of maturity that we all might strive for: "Among the Senoi, the terror dream, the anxiety dream, and the simple pleasure dream, as well as the muddled dreams of vague inconsequential happenings . . . largely disappear before puberty. From puberty on, the dream life becomes less and less fantastic and irrational, and more and more like reflective thinking, problem solving, exploration of unknown things or people . . ."

Moral: Life can be the stuff of which dreams are made.

Creative Alternatives Offer Choices

Mayor Moon Landrieu of New Orleans once told of a man who stumbled and fell over a cliff. On the way down he grabbed hold of a tree limb and dangled there helplessly.

"Anybody up there?" he called.

After a short pause the voice of the Supreme Being answered, "Yes" and urged that those in trouble have faith. Then the voice advised him to let go of the limb. At this, the man asked a second question: "Anybody else up there?"

In times of trouble or when faced with a challenging situation of any sort, we instinctively look for alternatives. Depending on our past conditioning, we may seek only those alternatives which are comfortable and comforting rather than those which may bring about a creative solution to a problem. Both can be natural responses, but the first very often limits our ability to cope with problems, while the latter at least offers the promise of a change. Creative people tend to feel more comfortable with change. They see life as a series of opportunities.

The Roman philosopher Lucretius saw beyond that: "One nation rises to supreme power in the world while another declines, and in a brief space of time the sovereign people change, transmitting, like Marathon racers, the torch of life to some other that is to succeed them."

Moral: Change is inevitable. Make it a change for the better, rather than the worse.

In the golden age of the hippies, a lawyer found a briefcase under the seat of a telephone booth in a county courthouse. He opened the case and found no identification but a seemingly bizarre collection of items: a tie, a brassiere, a copy of a law book (the penal code) and hair clippers. The lawyer knew at once to whom the briefcase belonged. These items had become almost essential accouterments of that day's criminal lawyer. If the client was without a tie, he provided one; without brassiere, he had one. If a young man's hair was too long or unruly, he had the clippers ready. All three were creative alternatives to prevent the prejudices of judge and jury from dominating the court proceedings. Studies had shown, for example, that youngsters with long hair received sentences twice as severe as those given to "clean-cut," "well-groomed" kids. The same is often true today, with "crime in the streets" as compared with white-collar crime. The criminal lawyer knows that if you look "good," people will think you can't be all that bad. So they try to consider not only their client's legal problems but also, like an undertaker, the value of cosmetic effects.

It is often difficult to draw the line between creative alternatives and illegal excess. Our era seems to be plagued with politicians and businessmen who have tried to expedite things (the defense argument) or overstepped the law (the prosecutor's case). Often even a jury cannot make up its mind.

A 15-year-old California boy with an overwhelming desire to see relatives in England stowed away on a Pan Am jet and arrived in London. Getting back was another problem, and his father had to foot the bill for a $380 fare. The father told reporters that paying him back would cost the boy "a lot of allowances." Instead, the boy came up with creative alternatives: he sold an exclusive story about his adventure to a London newspaper for $200 and collected $100 for a television interview, with the promise of another $100 from the TV station. Net profit, $20. However, an additional effort on the boy's part was on the thin line between legal and illegal. In return for a promise not to publicize how he got to London via Pan Am, the airline agreed to forget the whole thing. Net profit, $400. It would be difficult to decide who was more misdirected: the boy, for pushing his luck so that instead of turning an "honest" profit he doubled "his" money—a "lesson" few 15-year-olds can handle; or Pan Am, confessing itself a pitiful, helpless giant and therefore unable to cope with the ingenuity of an aggressive, obviously resourceful young man. At least it should have known that if one adolescent can think of a "foolproof" method of stowing away, another, if challenged, could do something better.

IX
Solutions

Not All Solutions Are Rational

Through the excessive use of the slogan "male chauvinism," we have acquired some feeling for the term. However, its adoption was inappropriate. "Chauvinism" was derived from Nicolas Chauvin of Rochefort, France, a veteran soldier of the First Republic and the Empire, who retained a simpleminded devotion and attachment to Napoleon. Subsequently, during the 1830's, this excessiveness came to be ridiculed in vaudeville, caricature, and lampoon. "Chauvinism" came to mean any kind of ultranationalism or excessive patriotism. It is a wild perversion of this term which rationally permits the use of "male chauvinism."

Chauvinistic thinking is based upon stereotyped assumptions, overwhelmingly one-sided points of view. People guilty of this type of limited thinking will find it difficult to come up with creative solutions. They also make a further hidden assumption that they *really* know what "right" is: that which is on their side. This is a grave error which many professional and amateur advice givers and receivers make in assuming that one can know what the problem "really" is. They consider a solution only on the basis of "exactly" what the problem is. They also end up assigning a priority to a single aspect of the problem, and their "solution" is directed to that alone. Small wonder that this type of advice is inadequate for all concerned. Attention should be given to the importance assigned by the person involved. Then mutual consideration should be shown for adjusting priorities. This is why agreement between the adviser and receiver on preferences is an important step.

Would-be advisers often assign one goal to all problems: win and win big. The trouble with this attitude is that, in these cases, for every winner there is probably a loser. This is acceptable in games and sports, but in real life it does not usually work out that way. The aftermaths of World War I and World War II are instructive. In both cases Germany "lost" the war. In the first war, however, a defeated Germany was ground into the dust, making a second war almost inevitable. At the end of the second war, Germany was partitioned—but the area controlled by the Western allies was built up substantially with American aid until it became a viable independent power. Surely no one could argue that the course developed after the second war was more sensible than that used after the first.

The inexperienced adviser seeks only a "rational" approach. Sometimes "rational" is "irrational" to others. Most of us find the irrational difficult to deal with. We may even find it difficult to define, since there can be thin threads of reasoning running through the most illogical thoughts. Thus we had the United States talking of arranging $2.5 billion in aid to North Vietnam while trying to "bomb it back to the Stone Age." And North Vietnam insisting that the United States alone foot the bill, though other countries, notably Japan, were eager to offer even more liberal aid at the time. There was also a city destroyed so that it could be "saved." Mary McCarthy mirrored this topsy-turvy world in a mock letter to Dr. Henry Kissinger suggesting the bombing of Harvard: ". . . surely it would be better to have Widener Library flattened by a patriotic American pilot than some long-haired hippy who has no respect for the traditional values that have made this country great." Finally, we had the Watergate Affair, in which a number of highly placed men became hysterical and indulged in the most irrational (and illegal) acts to protect the country and the Constitution from their mortal enemies, the Democrats. Win/lose? Yes; but notice that in some situations all can be losers.

Many men still find a woman's reasoning irrational. Here we would have to define the word as "not governed by or according to reason."

However, when women combine emotions, reason and intuition in one package, they become very convincing. Few will deny that their "female" view of the world is more complete than the limited "reasoned" one.

For an example of how a woman intentionally used a man's conception of the irrational, consider the small manufacturer whose industry was infiltrated and actually being taken over by gangsters. The criminals' progress seemed irresistible, since they dealt in terror. One of the manufacturer's competitors had been machine-gunned to death for vainly seeking police protection from the takeover. Shortly after this episode, this small manufacturer's turn came. He was quietly informed that he had a new partner. What could he do to stop someone who was working from an apparent position of absolute strength? An appreciation of patterns of behavior, the foundation upon which negotiating is built, was tried as the countervailing strategy.

The manufacturer's ultimate instrument was his spouse, an accomplished amateur actress who knew that few men can understand an irrational and hysterical woman. It was proposed that she visit the gangster's office. She entered late one Friday evening, throwing things and crying that she would kill herself, that she would go to the President, Governor and Mayor rather than let her husband team up with a murderer and a crook. She finally swept out, leaving chaos behind. The couple waited anxiously over that weekend for a reaction. There was none. Months went by. The "new" partner was never heard from again. As had been hoped, the gangster could not even understand his own spouse when she was "irrational." He was too smart a businessman to ruin a "good" thing by getting involved in a minor enterprise with a "crazy" woman.

The Floors in Your Life

A man once had to visit a New York City government building. After he had finished his business in a 15th-floor office, he punched the "down" button and waited for the elevator. And waited. And waited. Finally he returned to the office and asked the receptionist if anything was wrong. "Oh," she said, "if you want to go down you have to go up." She explained that during the afternoon rush hour, the elevators bypassed certain floors going down, but made all stops going up. The city agency he had been visiting was the City Planning Commission.

Few of us devote much thought, let alone planning, to the possibility that by shifting levels we may arrive at more satisfactory ideas and solutions to our problems. We feel that we are being "practical" when we say, "There is something wrong with *it*. I'll have to fix *it*." Thus we let a mere object dictate the solution to our problem. Small wonder that we find ourselves wanting to kick a thing that won't be fixed. After all, it's been doing our thinking for us. It would be more beneficial if we asked and answered such questions as: "Do I need *it*?" "What are the better ways?" "Where are other methods?" Human progress, as we know it, has been built on finding new methods as well as new things. Yet, oddly, we often do not realize that solutions to mundane problems lie in taking a broader methodological view, finding a different level. It is sometimes necessary to go up if we wish to go down and down if we wish to go up. The problem determines whether we go down to a more basic level or up to a level that satisfies greater demands.

Where can we find an illustration from our daily life? You have probably noticed blind ads in the newspapers that ask, "Do you want to make lots of money?" Most people would think "Yes," but do not answer the ad. Those who do often find that making "lots of money" equals selling insurance. Many people at first find themselves immediate successes as insurance salesmen (everyone has some relatives or friends who will buy). However, as soon as their limited prospects are used up, they become instantly unemployed. A few realize early that the problem is not *selling* insurance but *motivating* people to buy. At first glance this may not seem a significant shift in levels but it is: from "What's in it for me?" to "Where do *you* benefit?" One young salesperson was not content with this, going on to a higher level of sending birthday cards to all clients and potential clients. When this proved effective he went still further; he designed birthday cards for insurance salespeople and advertised and sold them to the industry. He had risen step by step from selling a tangible item, an insurance policy, to selling an idea, goodwill.

When we talk of changing levels upward, we are not implying a value judgment. You may move to a more basic level and achieve more social good than you would if you attempted to achieve a "higher" ground. For example, there is Samuel Johnson's observation "Patriotism is the last refuge of a scoundrel."

Where would this example, the level of preserving life itself, be placed?:

> And, behold, I, even I, do bring a flood of waters upon the earth, to destroy all flesh, wherein is the breath of life, from under heaven; and every thing that is in the earth shall die.
>
> But with thee will I establish my covenant; and thou shalt come into the ark, thou, and thy sons, and thy wife, and thy sons' wives with thee.
>
> And of every living thing of all flesh, two of every sort shalt thou bring into the ark, to keep them alive with thee . . .

Let us consider this a starting level.

Fortunately, the choices we face in life are not usually between life and death, to start all over again, or even between profits and poverty, but rather in the degree to which we are willing to make sacrifices in hopes of improving the quality of our life. Sometimes, if we are flexible enough to change levels, we can achieve both quantity and quality in "this best of all possible worlds."

Now, in the business world, the Flick Reedy Company of Bensenville, Illinois, needed a large supply of water for emergency fire use. The company thought of water towers, but they are costly to build and keep up, and besides that, they are ugly. Shifting levels, the company thought of an indoor swimming pool. It could be big enough to hold the required amount of water, yet the cost would be half that of a water tower. Thus the company created a pool for employee and community use, enhancing its public image in the community while saving money. The company was so pleased with this solution that it created a backup supply of water in artificial lakes which it stocked with fish, creating new opportunities for fishing and canoeing.

This company also displayed its creative multilevel thinking by requesting "blue-collar" workers to wear white shirts on the job. Its assumption was correct: The workers were much more careful about dirtying white shirts than blue ones, on which the dirt did not show. As a result, they were more cautious on the job. The plant's safety record improved and insurance costs came down.

An idea of what one wants can greatly aid one in determining where and when to look for it.

Moral: Does your choice of level contain a flaw?

The Solution Determines the Approach

The following telephone conversation took place in a New York hospital:

"I'd like to inquire how Ethel Gross is feeling."

"I'll have to connect you with the fourth-floor nurse."

"Is this the fourth-floor nurse? I'd like to inquire how Ethel Gross is getting along."

"Her condition is fine."

"When will they take her off intravenous?"

"In a day or two."

"When can she be expected to get up and walk around?"

"Within four days."

"When can she be expected to go home?"

"No more than a week. May I tell Mrs. Gross who called and was so concerned?"

"It's not necessary. This is Mrs. Gross. My doctor wouldn't tell me a thing."

Certain situations may require an indirect approach.

Panhandlers have developed two general varieties of approaches: the Ancient Mariner type (indirect) who fixes you "with a glittering eye" and insists on telling a long tale of woe before he makes the inevitable request for assistance, and the direct type who says he needs a drink and wants a specific sum to augment his meager supply of cash. The first tries to enlist your sympathy but is likely only to arouse your suspicion; the second appeals to you as a fellow man of the world. Both approaches are only sometimes effective. Therefore, to increase his number of tries in the limited time available to raise the money, the panhandler must try to be efficient. One sure thing is that the direct approach saves both the panhandler and his victim a great deal of time, and a decision can be made in an instant.

Many people who do not wish to spend the time prefer the direct approach. It shows that the two sides have reached a certain rapport that can quickly be translated into a mutually beneficial decision. The Ancient Mariner is much less likely to succeed. In his self-centered method, *his* problems are the most important in the world. The person he is dealing with is not likely to agree unless he can empathize in some manner. Even then his response cannot be predicted. The Ancient Mariner wants only to take—he wants a handout and an emotional outlet for his problems. He also leaves himself open to attack by a sophisticated person who responds to the direct approach but has no sympathy with the Ancient Mariner's demand for deep personal involvement.

Senator William Proxmire, a proponent of the direct approach, was the Defense Department's gadfly when, for example, he constantly criticized the brass for using enlisted men as personal servants. This finally evoked a plaintive cry from the Secretary of the Army that he didn't want the Army Chief of Staff going home at 5 P.M. to mow his lawn. Proxmire fired back: "Generals making over fifty thousand dollars a year in salary and equivalent benefits shouldn't be running home at five o'clock. At that rank and pay, they should be putting in long hours like the farmers, businessmen and construction workers of this country. Furthermore, when these other Americans go home after a hard day's work, they have to mow their own lawns and carry out their own chores." Rubbing salt in the wound, Proxmire suggested that lawn-mowing might be "fine exercise" for the generals. "The military brass do not even pay for their homes, which they get rent-free. The least they could do would be to keep them up without charging the taxpayers again."

Early in the Cold War an agent for the U.S.S.R. received handsome fees for excellent spy work. Only later was it revealed that all of his information was received from military and quasimilitary published sources. He would write a postal card asking the sources to mail him all their leaflets. They would put him on their mailing list, and send everything. It is unfortunate that so few adopt this common-sense, direct approach, but often when people believe that they must have something that is very important to them, they feel that they must use complex methods in order to obtain it. Consider, for example, the indirect approach used to avoid embarrassment by a 63-year-old woman who called the New School for Social Research to ask if she was too old for the Crochet Workshop. The registrar assured her that there were even older students attending. She then asked if she could register for more than one course. Assured that she could, she asked to be put down for Aspects of Human Sexuality also.

When the direct approach sometimes goes wrong, this can be due to incorrect assumptions about another's attitudes. Once a young man organized a group of his friends into a brainstorming session to consider his uncle's problem. The uncle had a small business and felt threatened when a large chain opened a competing outlet nearby. After half a day, the group came up with a number of ideas that seemed to be workable. When the young man excitedly called his uncle to tell him what he had done for him, the uncle reacted angrily: "*What* gives you the right to share my problems with strangers?" With that he hung up the phone.

The uncle's anger might have been on two levels: the one he expressed verbally and the other on the level of his incorrect hidden assumption that these were merely "decisions by committee." He had misunderstood. What was being offered was suggestions, not solutions. Usually any person who alone is responsible for the failure or success of an enterprise is not likely to have a high regard for a solution agreed upon by a majority—one product of group thinking. Nietzsche observed long ago that madness is the exception in an individual and the rule with groups. Groups do not think as individuals do, and the advice that they may dispense is not likely to be tailored to the needs of a person with a problem, nor is it readily acceptable to him. For your personal problem, which would you prefer: "My experience has been . . ." or "It has been decided by the committee that . . ."? The personal experience is more direct.

The person-to-person direct approach can be used most effectively in many instances. William Zeckendorf applied this principle when he wanted anything badly enough. If a person had money or real estate, or whatever Zeckendorf desired, he would stay physically near that person until he had achieved his goal. If the party went to Florida, Zeckendorf would go along. If he went to Europe, Zeckendorf would accompany him. This tactic, performed with the proper sophistication, can give the other person great ego satisfaction. It communicates nonverbally but directly that (at least for the moment) there is no other person as important in the life of this successful man.

Moral: Life provides the problems; we provide the approach.

Crisis and Opportunity

When something threatens to disturb the equilibrium of your daily life, you have a problem; when you feel you have reached a turning point in life and your decisions involve your survival, you have a crisis on your hands. Crises do not usually arise overnight. They can be the culmination of a series of mistakes, hidden assumptions, inadequate solutions and many other factors, some controllable, some not. Seldom are crises the result of a single cause. The words "For want of a nail the shoe is lost, for want of a shoe the horse is lost, for want of a horse the rider is lost" led Benjamin Franklin to conclude that "a little neglect may breed great mischief." True, but as with most truisms, life is not that simple. A single material object (even money) is not likely in itself to create a crisis. Far more often the material things combine with personality insufficiencies to create difficulty. A most common insufficiency is failing to meet life's new problems with new solutions. Tony Jones, a magazine editor, has observed: "No part of life is safe from swift change. That demands resilience, a capacity that declines with age. The old slow down, their adaptability suffers, they become a burden because they are imprisoned in assumptions too set to modify and too retrograde to accommodate." Some do not wait for old age to slow them down. They unfortunately keep the assumptions they acquired in their youth throughout their life. Henry Ford was a good business example. Late in life he tried to run a billion-dollar corporation as he had his one-man operation he had started at age 40.

This resulted in chaos and great financial loss to the company until he was forced out and modern management practices were introduced by the younger Henry Ford.

Bank robbers as well as businesspeople have difficulty in knowing when to discard solutions that have worked in the past. This often leads to failures and sometimes to their apprehension. Willy Sutton, for example, dressed in uniforms—postmen's, policemen's or Western Union messengers'—to gain entrance to a bank before it opened. This was his modus operandi—a term often used by policemen to describe the set pattern of behavior followed by a seasoned criminal. In passing, it might be noted that time changes everything. Try to imagine today even Willy Sutton dressed as a Western Union messenger attempting to gain access to a bank before the opening or after the close of banking hours. He would be picked up immediately as a fraud or a nut, or on a technicality called an anachronism.

The Chinese write the word "crisis" by combining the signs for "danger" and "opportunity." This element of profit and risk combined often attracts the gambling types who are naturally crisis-prone. There can be great excitement and even pleasure in confronting a crisis, and many thrive upon it. However, even the most capable operator cannot arrange for a weekly crisis, and a great deal of time is wasted neglecting problems as they come up in order to have a full-blown crisis always on hand. Constant crises, no matter how resourcefully they are met, are not the mark of an accomplished man. They breed instability rather than order, and no person, business or government can long withstand them. We have too great a need for stability and order to put up with stop-start, crisis-laden decisions. Consider your ability to be able to provide a smooth and orderly transition from the outmoded solution to a new one that answers present needs.

Some people are very successful in handling crises they have not created. The younger Henry Ford managed this when he took over the reins of the Ford Motor Company in the 1940's and brought the company up to date. Much more dramatic was Winston Churchill's taking over the demoralized British government in 1940. Five years later his services were rewarded in a curious way: ". . . at the outset of this mighty battle, I acquired the chief power in the State . . . all of my enemies having surrendered . . . I was immediately dismissed

by the British electorate from all further conduct of their affairs."
Obviously Churchill felt he was entitled to a slight breather after all
of his accomplishments over a five-year period. But defeat by his own
people was "a bit much." The British voters were not interested in
the war—that was over. Now they wanted far-ranging social reforms
which the Labour Party was ready to provide. Later still, in 1951,
Labour ran out of steam, public opinion changed and Churchill once
again became Prime Minister, showing possibly that loyalty and affec-
tion are not dead—they just have a lower priority than the more basic
human needs to be well fed and secure.

Sometimes we try to solve crises by seeming to turn the clock back.
Our urgent need becomes trying to preserve the status quo. Time
does not respond to any human holding action. This does not work; it
can produce only staged effects. The return to America's historical
past has produced such romantically successful vacation spots as Wil-
liamsburg and Mystic Seaport. In such places, buildings, ships and
ways of life that existed in past eras are carefully reconstructed and
re-created. They don't really succeed in actually existing, any more
than Disneyland attempts to create a real world. However, they can
be appreciated for providing a very real pleasure and some awareness
of life as it once was.

Aside from a romantic need to view our past, a *necessity* to re-
create the past can sometimes arise. One business need befell the
Campbell Soup Company when automobiles gradually replaced the
horse as a means of locomotion. This ultimately caused a crisis at
Campbell's. With the horse severely reduced in numbers, so was that
byproduct, horse manure, the preferred growth medium for mushrooms. Unless something drastic was done, Campbell's line would
have one less soup: cream of mushroom. The problem was assigned
to an engineering firm, which solved it by re-creating a horse's ali-
mentary canal in a block-long building. Hay and other materials went
in at one end and horse manure came out at the other. It wasn't a real
horse and it wasn't real manure, but it met present-day needs. A
production method was found for saving mushrooms from product
extinction. This served Campbell's economic self-interest. What it
did for the mushrooms, no one knows. Their life, after all, cannot be
too rewarding. The mushroom has, however, served as a symbol. A

corporate executive was asked how it felt to be swallowed by a conglomerate. "It's rather like being a mushroom. First they keep you in the dark. Then they throw dung all over you. And then they can you."

Moral: The difference in a crisis between opportunity and danger is point of view.

X
Teaching

Teaching and Teachers

A Kentucky Congressman was threatened with the ultimate weapon that can be used against politicians. The lady who had divorced him a year earlier announced she would run against him in the 1974 Republican primary. "I think people need to know about candidates," she cooed before closing in for the kill. "I plan to speak out about honor and integrity and morality."

Some might envy the lady her double role as teacher: educating the public and providing her ex-husband with a lesson. Others might suggest that the "public" is usually uneducable, and husbands always are. Still others would deplore the punitive use of "facts" to get across a biased point of view. And it is depressing that people find it easier to say, "I'll teach him!" rather than quote from Isaiah, as Lyndon Johnson frequently did, "Come now, and let us reason together."

Styles for teaching, like styles for women's clothing, go in and out of fashion. The educational "reforms" that promised so much in the 1960's gave way to doubts in the 1970's and were quietly replaced. In the 1980's, new "reforms" swept the old ones aside. The one thing that probably will never go out of style is the teacher who can narrow the gap that inevitably exists between teacher and pupil. But this is also true of any life situation where too often maintaining the distance between individuals somehow seems more important than mutual communication. In a campaign speech, which usually is not the ideal vehicle for wisdom, Roy Jenkins of the British Labour Party congratulated then Prime Minister Edward Heath for "stubbornness or determination." But, he said, "The tragedy is that Mr. Heath does not accompany these qualities with judgment, persuasiveness or imagination to see across the chasm of disagreement into the minds of others who disagree with him."

Mr. Heath was not alone. More important than the energy gap and all the other gaps—real and imagined—that confront us every day is the inability of people to take even tentative steps to establish communication with their "opposites." Instead, they want to play games weighted in their favor. But there is no easy way to compel others to play. As the late impresario Sol Hurok once said, "When people don't want to come, nothing will stop them."

Moral: Who is the teacher depends on the lesson.

An Educational Plan

Of all the physical resources of the United States that are wasted or underutilized, the public schools stand high on the list. Senator Frank Church of Idaho called them "sleeping giants" because they shut down in mid-afternoon and remain silent and empty on weekends and during long summer vacations. Some cities have established community programs to help "the neighborhood school become a total community center for people of all ages and backgrounds, operating extended hours throughout the year." One director said his entire program could be accomplished for 1 percent of the school department's budget "because none of this money must go into bricks and mortar—the schools are already there . . ." Yet the program consisted of adult education, teen centers, vocational training, and cultural and athletic activities.

A similar waste is observable in people who have too much time on their hands and don't know what to do with it. After all, a great deal of money has been invested in them—for health and education, for example—yet their minds stand idle like so many schoolhouses with their potentials unrealized. The potential lies not so much in learning "leisure-time" activities, however pleasant and rewarding it is to learn new skills. Instead, it is in dismissing the idea that education must be "practical." After all, if you have not learned the basic skills needed to permit you to function in the business world, you should go back to Square One—business school or college. Education for an adult should have a broader purpose. Norman Cousins says, "The purpose of education, if I understand it correctly, is to create a higher sense of the possible than would occur naturally to the undifferentiated intellect."

Can the mind be taught to differentiate? Of course it can. Cousins continues: "It must mean developing a zestful capacity for dealing in abstractions and, indeed, for regarding abstractions as the prime terrain for exploration and discovery . . . No abstraction, of course, is as potentially hazardous or fruitful as the individual's knowledge of and access to himself. Education's job is to improve this access, the hoped-for effect being the recognition of new options. Freedom is options."

Training for Maturity

Some equate broad exposure to life's problems with maturity and say, "Experience is the best teacher." More often, experience makes our behavior in the future more predictable. A similar situation will provoke a similar response. There are many Peter Pans, who "won't grow up," in the business world.

M. J. Rossant, writing about the Equity Funding Corporation scandal, listed the many businesses, government agencies, and other institutions that should have known that something was wrong, yet were so hypnotized by the generous dividends Equity was declaring year after year that they made no attempt to find out what could be wrong. "The fact is that everyone relied on everyone else, never doing his own homework. . . . Every major scandal can boast the allegiance of prestigious investors; it is an essential ingredient for getting a stock off the launching pad and into orbit. . . . Canny promoters know that if they can persuade sophisticated investors like a Bristol or a Morgan Guaranty or a Ford [Foundation] to place shares in their portfolios, others will follow. So they go to inordinate lengths to woo institutions, which, being human, are prey to flattery and greed."

It's the children's old game of Follow the Leader. Adults at least should recognize that the leader's sole motivation is to try to do things none of the rest of the group can do. He is performing stunts, which is fun for a child, but not very prudent for an adult. Stunts, like lotteries, may pay off once in a while, but they have a decided disadvantage: they mislead the one performing them into thinking that there will be a continuing payoff. The results are depressing. The loss of large sums of money is bad enough, but much worse is the waste of exceptional talent and knowledge. Put to work in a cooperative effort, they should almost invariably produce a more rewarding result. But when a life situation is reduced to stunt man and his blind followers, the result is chaos.

The educator Melvin M. Tumin observed: "Schools assume that it is as easy and as natural for children to be honest as dishonest, courageous as cowardly, and generous as selfish. It may very well be that unless otherwise restrained or impelled, the self-seeking organism known as the child, not born with anything called conscience, will prefer self to others, security to danger, sameness to novelty, hogging rather than sharing, force rather than deliberation or persuasion, lies rather than truth." He added, ". . . conformity to a moral code is proportional to the stake you have in the social order which urges that code upon you."

This last statement seems to suggest that moral codes tend to preserve the status quo. Perhaps this is so, yet only on one level: that of the immature person responding to carrot-and-stick. Life on the mature level can be much more than that. It is neither a playpen nor a jungle. It becomes a society in which all have much to gain and little to lose from a communal effort that tries to benefit everyone.

Moral: Decide, are we born moral in a capricious society, or capricious in a moral society?

A Guide to Intuition

Intuition is an important element in the decision-making process. Today, we tend to regard it as a feminine trait. Some highly intelligent men make grave errors for lack of intuition. They are often bound to limiting rules of logic, models and verifiable outside criteria for guidance. In day-to-day situations, certainly, women have more confidence in using intuition. Most women have no qualms about making decisions simply on their momentary feelings. (Possibly the accepted right of a woman to change her mind gives her such confidence.)

Everyone has intuition. With understanding, confidence and guidance, it can be improved. There are many levels in understanding the intuitive process. The primary layer might be called "woman's intuition." A working definition for woman's intuition is that it consists of a half-conscious blend of innumerable minute observations. For example, our present culture provides a woman with greater tendencies to look for small details, which she observes more accurately than a man. She will quickly note if someone's heels are run down, hair roots need touching up, nail polish is chipped, cuticles are rough, hair overbleached, etc. What she is doing is evaluating nonverbal forms of communication. This ability is further expanded and strengthened in any parent who has brought up an infant and has had to communicate with the child for two years on a nonverbal basis. Parents have had to recognize, understand, and satisfy their children's every need without being able to verbally communicate with them.

When used generally, the term "intuition" is so broad that there are as many as 50 different working definitions. For example, an appealing definition is receiving from your unconscious a relationship with your accumulated past experiences. Kant regarded intuition as the source of all knowledge, and Spinoza said it was the direct understanding of final knowledge, perfect truth.

Where does that warm feeling that one is right without any empirical evidence come from? Susanne Langer in *Philosophy in a New Key* speaks of the ". . . depth of the mind where 'intuitions' are supposed to be born, without any midwife of symbols, without due process of thought, to fill the gaps in the edifice of discursive or 'rational' judgment."

Intuition is an inspirational factor. It can supplement "rational intellect" and give deep judgments which reveal solutions for action. Pope in his *Preface to the Works of Shakespeare* observed, "He seems to have known the world by intuition, to have looked through nature at one glance."

How does this ability to know through other than ordinary channels operate? It does not look for reasons which seek to prove, but rather for deep understanding with which to know and believe. We can appreciate that we are dealing with a mental process much more extensive than the simple term "women's intuition."

The intuitive process appears to have different levels:

Primary: "Woman's intuition" is response to one's immediate feelings. On a more intuitive level, people can, with less information, get the point more quickly.

Secondary: In artistic as well as scientific fields, the understanding of meaning and significance is enhanced by intuition. In research and analysis, intuition helps form the shadow upon which substance is built. The American physicist Percy Williams Bridgman has said, "The base of science is, after all, the feeling in our bones that what we have done is right."

No matter at what level of intuition you may be operating, the following suggestions can be of assistance.

1. Try to be in touch with your feelings. The more you rely upon your sensibilities, the stronger and more dependable they become. Almost every experienced negotiator and diplomat will attest to this.
2. Allow yourself to experience your deepest feelings. They should not be disassociated from intuition and decision.
3. Acquire experience and data. These serve as necessary ingredients in the exercise of intuition.
4. In specific application to individual problems, the following mental states are helpful:
   (a) freedom from worry;
   (b) freedom from competing problems;
   (c) relaxation—rest in many forms, in bed, in bath; and
   (d) no interruptions.

5. Jot down ideas as soon as possible. Some ideas come into the consciousness and are lost because they are not immediately evaluated or grasped.

A word of caution. Distinguish between intuition and reacting on the basis of a label or classification. Intuition helps one to bring all past experiences to apply to the moment of decision. Reacting to labels works in the reverse. Here one has had only a few limited experiences and is projecting them as a general classification into future action. An example of this is a woman who says: "All men are the same. I know. I am married to one."

Problems for Advisers and Self-Advisers

As a frequent giver of advice, I attempt to "tailor-make" advice to suit the strengths and weaknesses of the person asking for it. Self-advisers must take special pains to ensure that they do the same. The secret is not to choose the "best" strategy, but to have a variety of creative alternatives to turn to when the assumptions you have made about your opposer turn out to be wrong.

It would be safe to say that most of those who seek professional advice have already tried the "best" way and run out of steam when it didn't work. Two experiences of mine can serve as examples:

Three San Francisco doctors once attended my Art of Negotiating® seminar shortly after they had led a work stoppage to protest ballooning malpractice insurance rates. For a week, San Francisco doctors refused to treat patients. I asked them what the public's reaction was and was not surprised to hear it had been awful—a public relations disaster. Then I asked if they had considered an alternative: Treat their patients without charge. Then they would have been the "good guys," protecting the public against the greedy insurance companies and rising medical costs.

It had never entered their minds.

My friend was leaving for the Continent, and we discussed being able to make successful deals. He said, "Look, if you're talking about large business enterprises, okay, but I can't even get a square deal in a small restaurant in Spain."

"Why not?" I asked.

"Well," he said, "the bill that I get never represents the prices on the menu." He asked if I had any suggestions for that.

I said, "Why not try this? When you've ordered the meal, hold on to the menu. Sit on it. Don't give it back. Then, when the check comes, compare the two, and at least you'll have the correct prices for what you ordered."

Thinking this pretty good advice, he went off to Europe. Many weeks later, I bumped into him and asked how the trip had been. He said it was wonderful, then added, "You know the advice that you gave me worked out very interestingly."

"It did?"

"Yes, I followed everything you said to the letter. I kept the menu, sat on it, and when the check came, I pulled it out and compared its prices with those on the check. Sure enough, there was a world of difference. I called the waiter over, but he interrupted me. 'I don't speak English.'

"Then the owner came over and listened patiently to my complaint. He immediately apologized for the mistake. There was obviously a big discrepancy between the bill and the menu prices. He would correct it. He whipped out his pen and changed all the prices on the menu."

In retrospect, I should have realized that my friend would not react to the owner's *fait accompli* as I would. He had already shown that in his past behaviour. His follow-through was not just weak, it was non-existent.

Moral: The proof of the pudding is in the eating, but then you have destroyed the proof.

Expert Advice

We expect experts to be able to teach us many things in areas where our knowledge is limited. Thus when the John Hancock Mutual Life Insurance Company decided to build its new headquarters building in Boston and make it the tallest building in New England, it turned to the distinguished architectural firm of I. M. Pei & Partners for design, to Purdue University for wind-tunnel tests and to contractors, subcontractors, and suppliers for their diverse expertise. The result: a 60-story building in Copley Square designed to have 10,348 Thermopane windows (costing $750 each) that would reflect historic buildings and open spaces. It was reported in *The New York Times* that the effect was somewhat diminished by acres of plywood that have replaced windows "broken, cracked, nicked, and apparently sucked out by the wind." Two thousand four hundred seventy-two windows had been shattered and 2,116 had suffered major damage, and every time the wind blew above 45 miles per hour, the police scrambled frantically to block off adjacent streets before more windows went. Although experts were consulted, they did not know why the plywood stayed on and why the existing windows had not blown out.

Moral: Experience can teach us lessons experts cannot predict.

We should limit our expectations of what an expert can or should do. After all, our important problems are made up of a number of smaller problems and dominant needs. We must accept the responsibility of fitting the pieces together to achieve a satisfactory solution. An expert can give answers to specific questions. He should not be burdened with making a choice that only you can make. Daniel S. Grenberg in *Saturday Review* made this point: "Secretary of War Stimson, toward the end of World War II, asked the leaders of the atom bomb project whether their creation should be used. Receiving the question at the end of a four-year, around-the-clock effort to build the bomb, they naturally replied in the affirmative." Not only did their own vested interests dictate a yes answer; they probably intuitively realized that Stimson wanted them to say yes, thus abdicating his own responsibility and spreading the blame around.

We should also retain our critical outlook when we deal with experts. They, like other mortals, are often incapable of viewing themselves objectively. One of the truly amazing things about Watergate is the number of lawyers who became involved and failed to furnish any moral guides. Or take the criticism by Judge David L. Bazelon in a speech before the American Psychiatric Association. He made these points about the psychiatric profession:

It operates behind a mystique created by the "closed doors of expertise."

It seems almost functionally incapable of initiating self-inquiry.

It makes decisions about patients not according to their medical needs but according to "hidden agendas" having to do with the doctors' perceptions of the good of an institution or a community.

It has no commonly accepted objective standards of good work, or any way to prove that psychiatric treatment really helps the patient.

These faults are not the exclusive possession of the psychiatric profession. They are shared in some degree by all experts. Used with precision, expert advice can be indispensable to making an appropriate decision. Used casually and carelessly, the advice of experts can be fatal to any enterprise.

Differences of Opinion Can Lead to Opportunities

A great many of us would be much happier if we could go through life wearing only one comfortable pair of shoes. Unfortunately, shoes wear out and styles change. So it is with opinions. Old opinions are comfortable. They don't have to be broken in. There are no painful pressures or pinching. They accommodate themselves easily to the quirks of our personality. Consequently, when new opinions are offered to us, we have a natural aversion to them.

In a way, this reaction is healthy. If we accept a new opinion, as we so often do, this will probably be the first and last time, before we reluctantly discard it, that we will examine it critically to see how well it suits us. Once we have made the choice, however, we can expect others to differ with us on the wiseness of our decision, just as others will cheer us on. This too is good for us, since our opinions mold much of our behavior and thought. And opinions in turn are based upon our assumptions of what is fact. Ideally, opinions should be constructed as carefully as a scientist builds up his hypotheses, always mindful of his assumptions and willing to leave open options for change. Few of us are so careful. We are more likely to adopt our opinions for the same reason children adopt stray cats and dogs—because "it followed me all the way home even when I tried to chase it." Therefore, we need the constant challenge of conflicting opinions to force us into a critical evaluation of our underlying assumptions and ideas.

When differing opinions are evaluated, they provide viewpoints by which we can see life through different attitudes on different levels by different means. When they are not valued, our lives tend to assume a rigidity that does little to enhance our possibilities of living a fuller life. Take for example the Frenchman whose opinion was that nothing should stand between him and a good meal. In July 1973, according to Agence France-Presse, he went to one of Grenoble's finest restaurants, dined well, washed his meal down with Nuits-Saint-Georges and topped it off with an old cognac and some champagne. Then he informed the waiter that he had no money. Amazingly, in the previous 20 years he had been convicted of the same offense 47 times and had served a total of 17 years in prison. The article concludes: "Right now he is back to his normal fare at the Varces-Grenoble jail." What feasts he might have had, had he given different opinions equal time!

XI
Learning

Talented Learning

It can be argued that teaching is a more limited process than learning. All too often teachers impose limits on what and how much they can teach, and their success or failure is very hard to evaluate either subjectively or objectively. Then, too, the teacher is usually considered knowledgeable in only one area of human thought. Some payers of school taxes positively insist that this be so, as any teacher who has advocated an unpopular cause can confirm. Ideas and options are often limited by the pressure of public opinion. Religious leaders also feel the pressure to teach "only what they know." Some even seem to take actual pride in their avoidance of the great social issues of our time.

Learning, however, does not suffer from these outside impositions. In fact, there is no real limit, except the length of our lives, to how much we can learn.

There can be self-assumed restrictions. For example, the muscles of the human body have long been designated as voluntary and involuntary muscles. We could will our hand to reach for a drink, but once we had swallowed, our muscles were on their own. The body could influence blood pressure, pulse rate, digestion, and so forth, but *we* could not. Now we are learning that we can will our involuntary muscles to respond to our direction. This new field of biofeedback (new to the West, at least; the East has known about its results for centuries) offers us a vast opportunity to learn, which we have only just begun to explore.

Even today the traditional fields of learning still offer us ever-increasing numbers of methods and ideas that we can, if we wish, try to learn. Somehow we must select and evaluate to find the ideas that are most useful to us, and this too is a learning process. A telephone company official, talking about wiretapping, observed that many customers who complained about taps called the phone company on the very instrument they suspected was tapped. Naturally, nothing was thereafter found to support their suspicion. When will *they* ever learn? Their idea may be right, but they don't know how to verify it.

Look to See—The World Is Yours

Psychologist George Miller says you can't hold more than about seven things in your mind at once. In his paper "The Magical Number Seven Plus or Minus Two," he reported that the number of dots people can enumerate at a glance, the random numbers they can remember, and the loud sounds they can distinguish all cluster around seven. He also points out that the seven items our attention span can encompass need not be all dots, sounds or numbers. They can be more abstract—for example, seven books. There are many people and projects that succeed with a number far less than seven. The "magical number three" might even apply to them. Who ever heard of being granted seven wishes? Or life, liberty, the pursuit of happiness, and four other items? The first three are quite enough to keep us involved for a lifetime.

To handle the many impulses received from the outside world, people must learn to deal in abstractions. They take a number of small and perhaps, to others, insignificant details gathered from their observations around them and weld them together into a new and workable whole. Usually they pursue their idea with single-minded attention over a given period of time. An unhappy example of single-mindedness was the man who went into a Newark bank to get a loan. When he was refused, he pursued his idea that banks are where the money's at. He went outside to the loading platform and picked up a bag of currency from the dolly of a Brink's truck. He was shot.

Far more successful was Oscar S. Wyatt, Jr., who formed Coastal States Gas in 1955. He observed and added the less important. The reporter Martin Waldron tells how Wyatt acquired $500 million:

> Mr Wyatt had an idea that the natural gas from junk wells in South Texas could be exploited. These wells normally do not produce enough gas to pay for laying pipelines to them.
>
> It was Mr. Wyatt's belief that if enough of these low-producing wells were tied together by small diameter pipelines, enough gas could be delivered to make it pay.
>
> Several South Texas towns agreed to buy gas at 20 cents per thousand cubic feet if Mr. Wyatt could deliver it, and the owners of 80 or 90 of the junk wells agreed to sell him their gas for 16 cents a thousand cubic feet. Mr. Wyatt used the 4-cent differential as the collateral for a $125,000 loan to put in his first pipeline

Moral: Small things added together can produce a big deal.

Don't Be Absorbed—Concentrate

Dr. Johnson once observed: "Depend upon it, sir, when a man knows he is to be hanged in a fortnight, it concentrates his mind wonderfully." A kiss, on the other hand, may cause a person to close his eyes. He is then absorbed in what he is doing. And so is a nursing baby. If it opens its eyes and begins to look at something, it stops sucking.

A clue to the difference between concentration and absorption is the prepositions used with their verb forms. We concentrate *on;* we are absorbed *in.* The concentration is involved with the world and the stimuli that constantly impinge upon our senses. The mind, however, selects the stimuli that are relevant to the thoughts at hand and rejects the irrelevant ones. By concentrating, we can choose and group the diverse stimuli of the world and create a different ordered whole. Thus we move to new discoveries about the world.

Absorption, however, closes off the world, and a person becomes preoccupied with a single element or process. In his monomania, he cannot move, because there is nothing to move to. His desire is to react to the same stimulus in the same way each time he encounters it.

In writing about chess, Fairfield W. Hoban relates that in 1920 Akiba Rubinstein, the Polish grand master, was absorbed in working out a difficult combination. At adjournment time, he went into the hotel dining room and ate a full-course dinner. When he had finished, he went into the lounge, then suddenly stopped, wrinkling his brow. It appeared that he was supposed to do something and he couldn't remember what it was.. He looked at his watch. He realized immediately that it was dinnertime. He went into the same dining room, sat at the same table, ordered the same meal from the same baffled waiter.

On the other side of the coin, a master swordsman tested his three best samurai disciples to see which one should succeed him. He balanced a pillow over the door so that when each one entered, the pillow would fall on him. The first to enter stabbed the pillow as it hit the floor. The second slashed it in two in midair. The third—who became the master's successor—did not enter the room. He sensed the trick that was about to be played on him. Many of us react to life by stabbing and slashing without evaluating whether the object is an "enemy" or a straw man. Some take pride in their lightning reaction. Others concentrate on the situation and thus can better determine if they should act at all.

We Are Not Taught, We Learn

When people come away from an experience with their own information and feelings rearranged, they have undergone a learning experience. Socrates with his dialectic method attempted by asking questions to get the answerer to reexamine their own thoughts and ideas, to order them, and to come up with new concepts that offered a broader view of life. Socrates attempted to have his disciples learn by guiding their experiences. Thus, "telling," which most of us assume is a proper function of a teacher, is not overtly used at all. Nonetheless, questions are a powerful tool for steering another's mind in the direction in which the questioner wants it to go. Sometimes it is effective. Sometimes it isn't. An English professor who was partial to the dialectic teaching method had this not-too-satisfactory dialogue with a student:

> "Miss Jones, would you give us your thoughts about the Man on the Hill in *Tom Jones?*"
> "Well, I thought he was very profound."
> "What do you mean, 'profound'?"
> "Well, he had a generalized concept of humanity, and I consider that profundity."
> "Would you say, then, that any man's concept of humanity is profound?"
> "It all depends on what you mean by any man."

Result: a breakdown in communication as the Socratic dialogue runs headlong into the Aristotelian "Define your terms."

Before we can learn, we must unlearn concepts that are inconsistent with new material that we encounter. We must bring old concepts to the conscious mind before we can change them, and even when we have done that, the old idea will have left an indelible mark on our unconscious mind that may distort the thinking process.

Learn to Make Mistakes

"They laughed when I sat down at the piano . . ." was the headline of a highly successful ad many years ago. It plays on the universal human desire to be an instant expert. Learning, however, does not usually come so easily. We must make mistakes in order to master any subject. More important, we must bring our vague feelings that we have done something incorrectly to awareness so that we can analyze what we did wrong and how we did it wrong.

So many vague attempts at teaching consist of saying, "You'll know you've done it right when it *feels* right." Even in the old artillery practice of bracketing—shooting over the target, under the target, then on target—you had to know where the target was. If you don't even know how it "feels" when it's wrong, how can you possibly know what the right "feel" is?

Some people go through life determined not to make mistakes. This is an inherently limiting attitude. They acquire a vested interest in concealing their mistakes and disguising them as virtues. Andrew Johnson was one of the least effective Presidents of the United States. There were many reasons for this, and most were beyond Johnson's control. But in *The Impeachment and Trial of Andrew Johnson,* Michael L. Benedict offers this insight: "Having taken a position on any issue, Johnson interpreted every attack upon that position as an attack upon himself. Rarely has a politician evidenced such personal involvement in his policies." In other words, he could not benefit from his mistakes because he refused to admit that he had made any.

When we bring our mistakes to the conscious level, we are then able to deal with them. Some can merely be eliminated. However, they can be replaced by a new pattern at the same time. Merely stopping such conduct is not in itself important. Destroying and replacing it can bring about a meaningful long-term change.

Learning from Misfortune

The ancient Greek playwright Aeschylus was the first to state that "Wisdom comes through suffering." Success alone does not make us wise. It often makes us careless. No one argues with success. Everyone, including the person who succeeds, is swept along on a wave of euphoria that does not really end until misfortune administers a sharp jolt. Then perhaps more realistic goals can be adopted.

A person whom misfortune has visited might profit from asking himself what, when/where, who, how, and why questions like these:

> What will I do from now on?
> When can I begin again?
> Where and when did my planning go wrong?
> Who else was at fault?
> How did it go wrong?
> Why did I get involved?

Honest answers to these questions won't prevent misfortunes from happening in the future, but they will make you wiser and less likely to repeat the same mistakes.

Just as some people are accident-prone, others keep attracting disaster because they fail to rethink and evaluate their past mistakes. If one becomes an observer who is prepared to learn by the unfortunate experience, the process can be like watching a ball game you have just lost replayed on TV in slow motion. A letter to "Dear Abby" gives a fine insight into how someone courts disaster:

> My problem is driving me up a wall. I met a most charming lady about six months ago . . . and we were headed straight for matrimony when I discovered we had a few differences. . . .
>
> She wants to live way up North. I prefer the South. She is a real swinger and likes to be on the go all the time. . . . I don't care to go out that much.
>
> She loves people and never met a stranger. It takes me a while to warm up to people. Her overly friendly ways, plus her D cup, which she flaunts a lot, has led her into a lot of trouble. She does have the gift of forgiving and forgetting, which I do not have.
>
> When I pointed out our differences, she offered to fix me up with some of her girlfriends, which I didn't go for.
>
> She says she loves me and wants to marry me, but I would have to change my ways. I don't think I could. . . . What do you think the chances of a successful marriage are between us?

To many men, marching down the aisle with this lady could lead to connubial bliss. For this disaster-prone gentleman who seeks to use "Dear Abby" as an expert, it would lead straight to the scaffold. He has stated all of the pieces of the "past" problems; he needs to make a decision, but lacks the wisdom to put them together properly. He must walk blindly toward disaster, and when he encounters it, hopefully he might learn. Of course, wisdom can come too late to be of much use. Nathan Horwitt, a mushroom expert, has said that *Amanita phalloides,* the deadliest of all mushrooms, is possibly the tastiest. Asked how he knew this, he explained that the poison is slow-acting and that often the first symptom of poisoning is communicated when the victim remarks, "Last night I ate the most delicious mushroom of my life."

Functioning Intelligently

We can gain new insight into intelligence by viewing it on three hi-
erarchical levels. First comes smartness—the ability of a "brainy" student to feed back to the teacher exactly what he has been taught.
Second is shrewdness. This is a level on which self-interest is dominant in meeting different life situations. The final and highest type of
intelligence is wisdom. It might be defined as shrewdness governed
by an extensive life philosophy. William Cowper points out the difference in a charming verse:

> I praise the Frenchman [La Bruyère], his remark was shrewd
> How sweet, how passing sweet, is solitude!
> But grant me still a friend in my retreat
> Whom I may whisper—solitude is sweet.

The three levels of intelligence are in many degrees interrelated.
A degree of smartness, the ability to comprehend, and even the ability to evaluate certain elements are needed for shrewdness, in which
things are learned not from a lesson plan but from life experiences.
Wisdom implies that a person not only has an ability to evaluate but
had developed a system of evaluation that is relevant and consistent.
The system is used to understand situations, anticipate consequences, and come to meaningful and harmonious judgments.

This letter appeared in *The New York Times:*

> Let the readers of your July 12 [1973] news article "Shrinking Dollar
> Pinches U.S. Tourists in Europe" beware of supposedly weak Scotch
> whisky in London—70 proof as compared to the 86 American proof.
> American-proof spirit is a mixture of half alcohol and half water by
> volume at a certain specified temperature; British-proof spirit is a mix-
> ture of approximately half alcohol with water by weight at another par-
> ticular temperature. Since alcohol is lighter than water, British-proof
> spirit is 57.06 per cent alcohol by volume, and therefore 70-proof Brit-
> ish is the equivalent of approximately 80-proof American.

This is the shrewd man talking to the smart man. The wise man
would no doubt have found that the different wallop Scotch had was
related to time, place, and company.

In any age there is no dearth of "smart young men." One told the Senate Watergate Committee that he had not revealed his bosses' wrongdoing "probably because of the fear of group pressure that would ensue, of not being a team player." Unfortunately, smart young men like to play games. Professors Thomas Franck and Edward Weisband noted that shrewd men played the game but played it differently: "Roger Hilsman, a former Assistant Secretary of State, in his book, *To Move a Nation*, did criticize Vietnam policies after waiting almost three years after his resignation and then did it in rather muted tones." They continue by pointing out that "of approximately two thousand men and women who have served in the Federal Government [in the 20th century] at, or above, the rank of Assistant Secretary or in senior positions in the White House, fewer than forty resigned and publicly criticized a policy with which they disagreed."

Although William Jennings Bryan did many things that might not be considered wise in the conventional meaning of the word, even in the Scopes trial he was totally consistent with the life philosophy that he had adopted. He was also consistent, in 1915, when he resigned as Secretary of State to protest President Wilson's bellicose notes to Germany. Franck and Weisband write: "Just before the break, Wilson sent his son-in-law . . . to try to convince Bryan to be a team player. He warned the Great Commoner that his public career would end if he resigned and went public. 'I believe you are right,' Bryan said. 'I think this will destroy me; but whether it does or not, I must do my duty, according to my conscience.'"

Today we are inclined to laugh at such sentiments. But is the smart team player or shrewd life player really that much better off?

Differing Views Of Religious Freedom

(1) Ladies First

> "Pat has a big book. Pat reads the big book. Jim reads the big book. Pat reads to Jim. Jim cooks." So begins the riveting tale of how a girl named Pat and a boy named Jim make raisin pudding and ham and tomato on toast.

Do you feel the foundations of the Republic shaking? Do you sense the faith of your fathers crumbling about your ears? Well, you should. You have just been exposed to a noxious influence called secular humanism. At least that's what Robert B. Mozert, Jr., of Church Hills, TN believes.

What's noxious about Jim cooking, in a primary school reader? The fact that Jim cooks *first*, before Pat, gives first-graders the idea "that there are no God-given roles for the different sexes." And that's not the only thing that people like Mr. Mozert regard as anti-God, anti-American and anti-family. Holt Basic Reading, a series of state-approved textbooks, also mentions evolution and a few of the world's religions.

It also shows some international communications symbols like the Olympic Games' designations for lunchroom (a cup and saucer) and first aid (a hand with one finger bandaged). These symbols, it seems, constitute an endorsement of nonverbal communication, which is a component of something fearsome called "new-age religion."

It's all so threatening that Mr. Mozert felt a duty to sue the county schools. He and COBS (Citizens Organized for Better Schools) say the Holt textbook series promotes secular humanism, and that the school system's refusal to provide an alternate violates the First Amendment rights of fundamentalist children.

This is no isolated case of know-nothing alarmism. In Mobile, AL, more than 600 fundamentalist parents, students, and teachers, joined by Gov. George Wallace, say secular humanism is a religion and should be treated like one. A "strict neutrality concept," one of their lawyers contends, "has already been equally applied to remove Judaism and Christianity from the schools. We're asking that it be equally applied to remove humanism."

A Federal judge, Brevard Hand, agrees. "It is time to recognize," the judge says, "that the constitutional definition of religions encompasses more than Christianity, and prohibits as well the establishment of a secular religion."

If the Alabama State Board of Education capitulates to the plaintiffs today (the local board has already done so) and the parents who have risen to its defense don't take up the suit, the Federal court will have gained the authority to approve or reject textbooks.

And screening them for signs of secular humanism could mean the removal of anything—from a discussion of economics that explores the weaknesses as well as strengths of capitalism to all that stealthy E.R.A. propaganda in stories about little boys who make raisin pudding.

Since what is anti-God, anti-American, and anti-family could be whatever a vocal minority says it is, tomorrow's textbooks might be pretty slim. That should suit that minority very well. Why mess up a kid's head with information when ignorance of secular humanism, and much else besides, is all the armor anybody needs?

—An editorial in *The Washington Post*, March 13, 1986

Moral: According to Mr. Mozert, every living thing has a God-given role. For example:

"Nature has given horns to bulls, hoofs to horses, swiftness to hares, the power of swimming to fishes, of flying to birds, understanding to men. She had nothing left for women."

—Anacreon, *c*. 500 B.C.

Translation: A woman's place is in the home.

(2) The Violation of a Sanctuary

Harvey Cox, a theologian and a member of the Old Cambridge (Mass.) Baptist Church, wrote in *The New York Times* (March 3, 1986):

Last Sunday, the minister of the small Baptist church I belong to did a very nice thing. During the pastoral prayer, along with remembering the sick and the shut-ins, he also asked the Lord to bestow a special blessing on our informer.

Now, a visitor might have thought that sounded a bit odd. But we knew what he was talking about. It has recently come to light that the Government has been placing investigators with body bugs in churches helping refugees from El Salvador, or thinking about doing it.

In our case, the Government has been considerate enough to tell us we had an informer. It happened like this. Last spring, when we heard that some other churches were doing the same thing, we wrote to Washington asking for whatever files the Government might have under the Freedom of Information Act. The Government told us it was very sorry but that it could not send us the files because they might "reveal the identity of an individual who has furnished information to the F.B.I. under confidential circumstances."

Cox noted that other churches have brought a suit asking the government to forbid such activities as a violation of the Constitution. However, it would probably take five years to reach the Supreme Court. The article closed on this optimistic note:

Five years is a long time to live with electronic eavesdroppers in the pews. Still, in the meantime, I am glad our preacher asked the Lord to grant a special blessing to the informer. In fact, we all secretly hope our infiltrator does not get tired and quit. If he stays around long enough, he'll learn that when we say our church is a "sanctuary," we don't mean just for Salvadoran refugees. Churches are sanctuaries for homeless, lost and confused people of all kinds, including secret agents. They, too, are welcome to come and pray, listen to the Gospel reading and belt out "Beulah Land" with us. Who knows, they might even end up getting saved. It wouldn't be the first time.

Moral: "I believe in it [the Bible] first, because I am Bishop of Autun; and secondly, because I know nothing about it at all."

—Ascribed to Talleyrand

Apparently, neither does the secret agent, but perhaps he can learn.

Peace at Last

Some years ago, I was asked to chair a meeting of 200 peace groups. I asked, "Why me?" I was told the groups needed a peacemaker from the outside. They ranged all the way from extreme right to extreme left and in the past had had such fierce battles that nothing had been accomplished.

I accepted the challenge.

A week before the meeting, I was given the agenda. I knew immediately there would be trouble. The first item on the agenda asked each group to tell how it differed from the other groups.

I changed a few words and called the meeting to order. Then I asked each group to tell what points of agreement they all had in common.

It worked. I presided over the first meeting of the peace groups that reached unanimous agreement on a course of political action.

Moral: If you want a war, stress differences; peace, stress agreement.

XII
Things To Recognize In Advice

Human beings are born into cultures that provide them with methods for learning about present abilities and past achievements. It is not necessary for each new generation to discover fire or invent the wheel. Yet while "known" facts (and fallacies) are somewhat effortlessly transmitted from generation to generation, successful techniques for giving and receiving advice, one of the strongest socializing pro-cesses, is generally ignored or misused.

Our life experiences have supplied each of us with a variety of advice that we consider worth passing on. But when Edward, Duke of Windsor, looked back, in *A King's Story,* on a life rich in pomp and ceremony, all he could come up with was this: "Perhaps one of the only positive pieces of advice that I was ever given was that supplied by an old courtier who observed: 'Only two rules really count. Never miss an opportunity to relieve yourself; never miss a chance to rest your feet.' "

Or consider this advice given to Nelson Algren by a prison inmate:

Never play cards with a man called "Doc."
Never eat in a place called "Mom's."
Never sleep with a woman whose troubles are worse than your own.

We can't quarrel with these bits of advice. Possibly they are even good advice if you are a courtier or a criminal. But if you regard advice as a distillation of life experiences, the results in both cases are rather meager. Probably the problem is that both of these advice-givers have learned about the process in a rather haphazard manner. Receivers of advice also suffer from certain self-imposed limitations. In the first century B.C. Publilius Syrus wrote: "Many receive advice; few profit from it." The observation needs no updating. Now is the time to apply some of the stories, anecdotes, and "morals" to the advice process.

Unfortunately, we have all been given advice that was not helpful, and this has caused us arbitrarily to reject all advice from the suspect source. All too often the parent-and-child relationship is a good example of advice proffered and refused. Yet even when advice is meticulously followed, unsatisfactory and even disastrous results can occur. One reason is that givers of advice are not all equally motivated. Some givers may be motivated in opposition to receivers' needs. The professional, playing a role, may do it only for money; the friend, to engender gratitude or to place the other person in his or her debt; the stranger, to display superior knowledge and thus increase his or her self-importance; the parent, to establish dependency, to control, or perhaps to minimize a sense of self-guilt; the coach, to show superior knowledge of the game and to change the score, not to improve the players' performance.

How can anyone fully rely on what these advice-givers say? Most people are consciously or unconsciously aware of these mixed motivations and remain suspicious. Some lose their ability to choose and become dependent and helpless.

Receivers of advice have similar shortcomings. They sometimes seek advice only to reconfirm their preconceptions. They do not listen because the advice is uninteresting, already known, too complicated, or too simple.

One way of reversing the unhelpful aspects of the advice process is to become aware of the shortcomings and to view advice as a method in which both giver and receiver can learn from each other and grow. Advice *can* be made useful.

Advice most basically deals with human motivation, and that can be studied most readily by answering questions that begin with What; When/Where; Who; How; and Why. Rudyard Kipling calls them his "six honest serving men (They taught me all I knew)." Edmund Burke believed that the questions could cover every aspect of motivation in life situations.

Let's consider them briefly, for they are basic to all advice and any subject that is amenable to the advice process.

What

The advice process can be a personal one. You can be both the giver and receiver, and be open enough so that each role is made aware of the other. The environment can be defensive because we try to protect ourselves even from ourselves. We use every Freudian trick to achieve this.

Have you ever noticed how you react when you feel you are being taught? Compare this with being assisted to learn. The same is true with the advice process. Whether you are an amateur or a professional adviser, your function may be merely to stimulate thinking and point out alternatives. The individual has inner feelings and experiences that you cannot share merely through conversation. He or she has stayed awake, involved in personal problems, alone has had the experience and must take the consequences created by the problems. Even a professional is not required to become an instant expert when given a summary of a life experience, nor is likely to become one. He or she can't avoid viewing it as a generalized problem that requires a generalized answer, one that fits snugly into his or her area of expertise. More effective, perhaps, would be for the giver and receiver to offer alternatives so that the receiver gains insights into his or her habitual ways of handling problems and can evaluate them in comparison with different and possibly more effective approaches.

John Corry reported in *The New York Times* that one day a news dealer in lower Manhattan was shouting, "*Post! Post!* Get your *Post* here."

A man walked up and asked for the paper. "We're out of *Posts*," the news dealer told him.

"What are you yelling '*Post!*' for if you're out of them?"

The dealer shrugged. "Habit."

Moral: Let not the balance of your life rest on habit.

A common error in our consideration of advices is to divide it into "logical" opposites: black or white, yes or no, do this or don't do that. Life rarely affirms the strictly logical. In dealing with a problem, if you ever think that you have come up with the "best" or "only" answer, realize what has happened. You have subconsciously and consciously stopped thinking about your problem and therefore you have stopped looking for alternatives. Let us assume that you have indeed come up with the best or only answer. You may be sure that time will change all of that. Even before you use it, the answer may become outdated. Therefore, it is important to continue to keep an open mind about your problem and not limit yourself by concluding you have come up with the "best" and "only."

Advice we act upon helps to fulfill our expectations in accordance with our philosophies. It is necessary for us from time to time to reexamine our philosophy of how to handle life.

We all seem to have insights with which to handle daily problems. Unfortunately, some of these have been developed when we were children. They are left over from passing philosophical systems which we grew out of or discarded as inappropriate. In our present mature state, it is a good idea to reexamine our philosophies and see if we wish to continue to be governed by them. Some cynical philosophies have been expressed as "Do unto others and beat it," "Do unto others before they do it to you" or "I don't get mad, I get even." These philosophies are not of a type that most of us could reasonably subscribe to. However, it must be considered that they are philosophies that are present in certain people and have to be dealt with.

Moral: Philosophy flavors all advice.

When/Where

Time and place should be considered as one unit. Appreciation of the changes that continuously occur provides great insights. In some instances all that may be needed is to let time do the work. A young pianist felt that there was no fairness in the study of music. At each lesson her teacher would insist that she must practice more, despite her protests that she had been practicing diligently. "It wasn't enough," the teacher would always say. Finally the student became so outraged she didn't touch the piano all week. At her next lesson, she was astonished to find her playing had improved. "You see," the teacher said, "I told you that all you needed was more practice."

Now, when today's knowledge may become obsolete overnight, we can never be sure whether the experts we turn to for advice are giving us current "facts" or ancient history. Francis Bacon realized this when he wrote, "Ask counsel of both times: of the ancient time that is best; and of the latter time that is fittest."

Sometimes experts may even be giving us information that is too far ahead of its time to be considered appropriate. John L. Hess in an interview with Dr. Francois Jacob, Nobel Prize winner in medicine, touches on this, quoting Dr. Jacob: "When conditions are ripe, many scientists will be racing for the same answer, as when Darwin brought out his concept of evolution, and when the time is not ready, even the right answer will be ignored, as were for 35 years Mendel's great discoveries about heredity." So a third element is added to any problem we may try to solve: how do we know when the time is right? Again we rely on intuition, speculations, feelings, hunches, or merely guesses. Past experience has given us these clues as to when we have been ahead of the times, behind the times, and on time. This built-in clock tells a different time to each individual. It can be altered and perhaps improved, as can the process of receiving and acting on advice, by a conscious effort to expand the use we make of our past experience.

Who

In many of our life roles we act like animated tape recordings of the past. Often as parents we not only repeat the scripts our parents used but duplicate their gestures and tones of voice. Some escape one prison cell by locking themselves in another one. They reject their parents and repeat the script of what they told their favorite toy or their dog when they first reacted against parental authority. Thus they carry into new situations the childlike and self-indulgent feelings of the past.

A musician who has become accomplished may be called upon to teach. Then it may be difficult to explain the techniques that have become second nature to him or her. In despair he or she may resort to the exercises that a teacher once prescribed, even though they seemed of little value at the time. He or she tries to break down a fluent technique into fragmented parts. In turn, any talented student will rebel against this fragmentation. If the musician's new student finally achieves mastery it is through his or her own insights. Then he or she in turn finds it difficult to explain.

This dichotomy between life and art is clearly illustrated in the case of Jean-Claude Dague, a French specialist in directing gangster films. Because he could not get financial backing for a cops-and-robbers film, he turned to bank robbery for the money he needed. The wonder was that he robbed seven banks before he was arrested. Instead of imitating the slick, well-planned jobs depicted in his films, he and his accomplices used their own cars and didn't even bother to change the license plates. Dague was an expert at directing movies (doing the exercises), but he could not apply his artistic expertise (mastery) to a life situation.

Givers of advice face similar problems. All too often they suggest only those alternatives which they think have been effective in their previous life experiences. Because they have been successful, they think that their solutions are the only ones that work. This is a dangerous assumption. Certainly 30 years of experience does not mean that we have been successful for 30 years. We may merely be like the man who, when asked what he did during the French Revolution, said, "I survived."

How

In most life situations you are the expert. You are most familiar with the background, facts, and people involved. If you were to make a judgment as to what to do, it would probably be satisfactory if you had carefully considered the many alternatives available. This is where the professional expert can help you—the practical expert. Your thoughts should be stimulated. You should be given a touch-off point for your ideas. The materials offered should serve as catalysts to restructure your experiences and make them more meaningful. To be offered only the advice that seems "best" to the professional expert is a disservice to the receiver of advice. It fails to take advantage of your own experience and knowledge. Both giver and receiver of advice should consider themselves associates in the process. They should pool their facts, experience, and judgments to arrive at satisfactory solutions to problems that concern them both, but they should realize that their concern takes place on different levels.

Some years ago AT&T was advised that the next "great leap forward" would be the Picturephone—a telephone that lets you see as well as hear the person to whom you are talking. With much fanfare it was introduced in three cities. In 1974, AT&T disclosed that 12 customers had signed up in Pittsburgh but had later dropped out. Three signed up briefly in Washington, D.C. Only in Chicago, apparently, did anyone care to look at the person he or she was talking to—and even in that city there were fewer than 100. Ma Bell then appointed an assistant vice president in charge of Picturephones to come up with ideas on what potential customers really wanted to see. Years later it was tacitly assumed that the only thing customers wanted to see was lower rates.

Why

If your philosophy allows for free will, infinite determinism, or other alternative choices, then you must admit responsibility for your actions. Advice attempts to provide choices and experiences that will accelerate our desires and fulfill our needs. The choices we make are meaningful for the balance of our lives. We are satisfied or have learned or are disappointed. When next confronted with a similar experience, we choose an alternative that seems more likely to succeed and try to avoid disappointment. We usually do not ever again test the path that has led to bad results. This type of learning experience should be understood and utilized to a limited degree. However, we should be aware that similar experiences are not always the same old experiences. The differences between them can make a big difference. During the Senate hearings on the appointment of Gerald Ford as Vice President, Ford made this statement: "I learned long ago that after a play is called, you do not go out and tackle your quarterback." A short time later this "What, never? Well, hardly ever" exchange straight out of Gilbert and Sullivan took place:

Senator Harrison Williams objected to the application of football analogies to the governmental process. What, he asked, would Ford do if his quarterback got turned around and started running with the ball to the wrong goal line? "Wouldn't you tackle him?"

Ford recalled that such a situation had once actually occurred and added, "But that's the exception more than the rule."

"These are exceptional times," Williams told him.

Epilogue

This book was designed to show directions rather than point out individual paths.

Having a course gives people confidence in their choices. It utilizes their individual experiences, capacity, and skill to perform.

The foundation of advice is the good sense to share, fully and openly, the ability to understand, and to employ the full range of talents of all participants.

Humanity has much to share. May your advice point in that direction.

Index